Z

P

Produced by Mercy Khozi and Helen Rana
Cover photos by Helen Rana
Illustrations by Rabby Mwanza

First edition published in Zambia, 2000
This edition published in the UK, 2021

ISBN: 978-1-3999-0268-7

Contents

Preface

English is the official language of Zambia. There are seven local languages which are most widely spoken and understood in the country – Bemba, Kaonde, Lozi, Lunda, Luvale, Nyanja and Tonga. These languages are all included in this phrase book. There are also around seventy other languages or dialects spoken in Zambia, reflecting the large number of tribal groups living in the country.

This phrase book will enable you to get by in the local language – wherever you are in Zambia!

Pronounce the words exactly as they are written.

Acknowledgements

We are very grateful to the contributors of this book:
Bemba – D.C. Nkosha
Kaonde – H.L. Mabange, Amos Kombe, Bishop S. Kipaila
Lozi – Mukatimu Munalula
Lunda – Lydia Simeta, Kokoma Emmanuel
Luvale – Mr and Mrs S. Kapanji
Nyanja – Rabby Mwanza
Tonga – Maluba Hanhadu

We are also grateful to Professor Simwinga from the University of Zambia for editing the text.

BEMBA

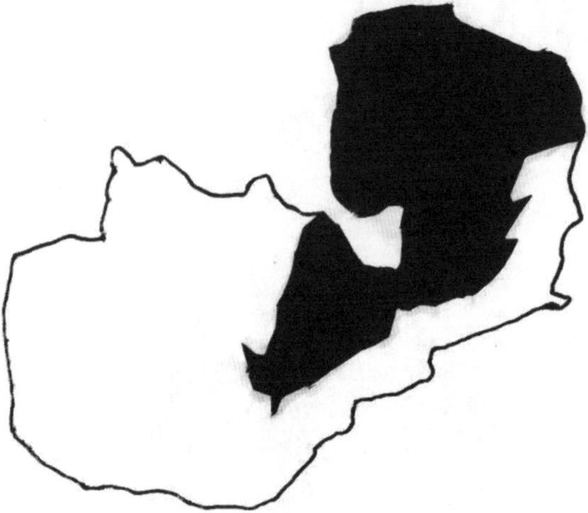

The Bemba-speaking people of Zambia live mainly in the Copperbelt, Central, Luapula and Northern Provinces.

'Bangilila, mulamba talaatulula'
Start early before the floods come

GREETINGS AND FIRST WORDS

Hello	Mwapoleeni
How are you?	Muli shaani?
I'm fine. And you?	Ndi bwino. Nga iwe?
Fine, thank you	Ndi bwino mukwai, naatasha
Good morning	Mwashibukeeni
Good afternoon	Icungulopo mukwai
Good night	Sendameenipo mukwai
Goodbye	Shaaleenipo
See you!	Twalaamonana!
Yes	Emukwai
No	Awee
Maybe	Nalimo
Okay/fine	Cilifye
Excuse me	Njeleleeniko
Sorry	Njeleleeniko
Thank you very much	Natotela saana
What's your name?	Niwe ani ishina?
My name is…	Ishina lyandi nine…
Pleased to meet you	Ciisuma twamonana
Please come in	Ingileeni mukwai
Please sit down	Ikaleeniko panshi mukwai
Welcome	Twamusekelela
Please can you help me?	Njafwilisheeniko mukwai?

Who?	Naani?
What?	Cinshi?
Where?	Kwi?
When?	Lilali?
Why?	Cinshi?
Which?	Cisa?
How?	Shaani?

To show respect, preface the name of the person you are talking to with 'Ba', e.g. May – Ba Mary; Mr Phiri – Ba Phiri.

GENERAL CONVERSATION

Do you speak English?	Bushe kuti walanda icisungu?
I don't speak Bemba	Nshilanda icibemba
I speak a little Bemba	Ndalanda icibemba panoono
I am learning Bemba	Ndeesambilila icibemba
Sorry, I don't understand	Nshileumfwa mukwai
Please repeat that	Bwekesheenipo mukwai
Please speak slowly	Landeeni panoono-panoono
What is this?	Cinshi ici?
How do you say… in Bemba?	Mulanda shaani… mu cibema?
How do you say… in English?	Mulanda shaani… mu cisungu?
Did I pronounce it right?	Bushe niinanda bwino?
Do you understand me?	Bushe muleengumfwa?
This is my…	Uyu…
Wife	Mukashi wandi
Husband	Umulume wandi
Son	Umwana wandi umwaume

Daughter	Umwana wandi unwanakashi
Sister	Nkashi inandi
Brother	Ndume inandi
Friend	Umunandi
Family	Ulupwa
I work as a…	Momba incito ya…
I am… years old	Ndi ne myaka…
Are you married?	Mwalwupwa?
I am married	Naalwupwa
I am not married	Nshaupwa
How many children do you have?	Mwakwata abaana banga?
I don't have any children	Nshakwata abaana nakalya
I have… children	Naakwata abaana…
I am on holiday	Ndi pa holiday
I am working here	Mibomba apa
I live here	Njikala apa
Where do you come from?	Mwafuma kwi?
I am from…	Naafuma ku…
Can I take a photo?	Kuti naamukopako?
Where is the toilet?	Icimbuusu cilikwi?
Entrance	Apakwingilila
Exit	Apakufumina
Ladies	Abaanakashi
Gentlemen	Abaume
Me	Ine
You (singular)	Iwe
You (plural)	Imwe
She	Umwanakashi
He	Umwaume
We	Ifwe

They	Ba
I feel cold/hot	Naumfwa impepo/ukukaba
I feel tired	Naumfwa ukunaka
I am hungry and thirsty	Ndeumfwa insala necilaka
Okay/fine	Bwino
I like it here	Naapatemwa pano
Mr	Ba
Mrs	Muka
Miss	Umushimbe
See you later	Twalaamonana
See you tomorrow	Tukamonana mailo
Why?	Cinshi?
Because…	Pantu…
I don't understand	Nshileumfwa
I don't know	Nshiishiibe
I think…	Ndeetontonkanya
I want…	Ndeefwaya
I don't want…	Nshileefwaya
I like…	Naatemwa
I don't like…	Nshatemwa

GETTING AROUND

Excuse me, where is…?	Nikwi, ukuli… mukwai?
Where are the…?	Nikwi ukuli…?
Shops	Amatuuka
Restaurants	Umwakuliila
Night clubs	Ku makalabu yabushiku
Where is the…?	Nikwi ukuli…?

English	Bemba
Lake	Bemba
River	Umumana
Village	Umushi
Game park	Uko basungila inama
Post Office	Post Office
Bank	Bank
Bureau de Change	Uko bacinja indalama
Museum	Museum
Church	Ku calici
Bus stop	Pa citesheni ca saaca
Train station	Pa citesheni ce shitima
Airport	Kucibansa candeke
Where is this?	Nikwi ukuli…?
Can I walk there?	Kuti naenda ukuya kulya?
Do you have a map?	Naamukwata maapu?
Can you show me?	Naangeeniko?
To the…	Pilibuka ku…
Left	Kuso
Right	Kulyo
Straight ahead	Kabiye pantanshi
Where are you going?	Nikwi uleeya?
I am going to…	Ndeeya ku…
Is this the way to…?	Bushe iyi enshila yaku…?
I want to travel by…	Ndeefwaya ukwenda…
Bicycle	Ne ncinga
Motorbike	Ne citukutuku
Boat	No bwato
Horse	Na kabaalwe
Vehicle (general)	Na motoka
How much does the journey cost?	Mulipila shinga pa bulendo?

How long will it take?	Calaasenda inshita nshi?
Can I buy a ticket?	Kuti naashita itikiti?
Where's the bus/train/plane/ boat for…?	Saaca ileeya kwi/ishitima lileeya kwi/indeke ileeya kwi/ubwato buleeya kwi?
How can I go there?	Kuti naaya shaani kulya?
I want to see the…	Ndeefwaya ukumona…
Is there a driver?	Ekwali namutekenya?
Is there an entrance fee?	Bushe kuulipila pakwingila?
What are the opening hours?	Beesula nshitanshi?
It's open from… to…	Beesula inshita ya… ukufika inshita ya…
Street/road	Umusebo
A little bit	Panoonofye
A lot	Ingi
Quickly	Bwangu
Slowly	Panoono
What's the best way to…?	Cinshi cingawamapo uku…?
Should I take a taxi?	Bushe ndeeya natakisi?
It's near the …	Mupeepi naa…
Cross the road	Ciluka umusebo
Go past the…	Mupite pa…
It's near here	Nimupeepi naapa
It's far from here	Paatali ukufuma kuno
It's too far to walk	Paatali teekuti mwende
It's ten minutes by foot	Cisenda baminiti ikumi nga kwendafye
It's five minutes by car	Cisenda bamniti basaano na nimootoka
Do I need my passport?	Bushe passport ileefwaikwa?

PUBLIC TRANSPORT

Is this the right bus for…?	Bushe uyu esaaca aya ku…?
Where's the nearest bus stop?	Nicisa icitesheni ica saaca icabeela mupeepi?
How much is the fare?	Mulipila shinga apa?
I'm going to…	Ndeya ku…
Where can I drop off?	Naalaikilila pii?
Which bus/train can I take to…?	Nisaacanshi/liishitimanshi ninganiina ukuya ku…?
Can I have my change?	Mpeeniko changi yandi?
Please stop here	Iminina apapeene

CARS

I want to hire a car	Ndeefwaya ukwashima mootoka iyakulipila
Where's the best place to rent a car?	Nikwi ukusuma uoko ninga shima mootoka?
I want a small/large vehicle	Ndeefwaya mootoka iinoono/iikalamba
I want it today/tomorrow	Ndeifwaya ileelo/mailo
How much do you charge?	Mulipilisha shinga?
Fill it up please	Isusheeni
The tyre's flat	Itayala lyapompoloka
It's broken down	Naifwa
Can you fix it?	Kuti mwalungisha?
Is there a garage/mechanic near here?	Bushe kuli uwaishiba ukulungisha pano?

When will it be ready?	Mukapwisha liilali?
Can you do it now?	Kuti walungisha nomba-liine?

GAME VIEWING

We want to go somewhere on Friday	Tuleefwaya ukuya kumo pali cisaano
There'll be two of us	Tukabafye babili
Is it worth seeing?	Bushe kusuma?
Is it suitable for children?	Bushe abaana abanoono kuti basangwako?
How much does it cost?	Kuulipila shinga?
What does the price include?	Bushe muli uyu mutengo finshi finbi ifipendelwamo?
What time will we leave?	Tuleeya nshitanshi?
What time will we get back?	Bushe tuleebwela nshitanshi?
Is lunch included?	Bushe ne cakulya cakasuba naacipendelwako?
Where do I buy a ticket?	Nikwi ningashita itikiti?
Buffalo	Imboo
Crocodile	Ing'wena
Elephant	Insofu
Giraffe	Indya-buluba
Hippopotamus	Imfubu
Lion	Inkalamo
Monkey	Kolwe
Rhinoceros	Icipembele
Snake	Insoka
Zebra	Coolwa

AT THE HOTEL

I want a good hotel	Ndeefwaya iotelo ilisuma
Do you have a room available?	Naamukwata incende yakulaalamo?
I want a room for… people	Ndeefwaya umuputule… wabantu
With a nice view	Ukuleemoneka bwino
For one night/two nights/ one week	Ubushiku bumo/ishiku shibili/ umulungu umo
I've made a reservation	Niisungisha incende
My name is…	Ishina lyandi nine…
How much is a room?	Nishinga umuputule umo?
Is breakfast included?	Bushe umwikulo naupendelwako?
Is it air conditioned?	Mulapita umwela?
You are in room number…	Muli mumuputule namba shaani…
Please give me a wake-up call at	Mumbuushe inshita
Is there a restaurant here?	Bushe pali mwakulila pano?
Is there a…	Bushe kuli nee…
Swimming pool	Icishiba cakoowamo
Gym	Umuputule wakwangalilamo
Hairdressers	Kusaluni
Gift shop	Ituuka lyo bashitamo ifyabupe
Night club	Kalabu yabushiku
Business centre	Incende yamakwebo
Room service	Ifyakuliila mu muputule
Please bring… to my room	Mukwai muleete ku muputule wandi…

Please bring my luggage	Mukwai muleete icipe candi
Are there any messages for me?	Bushe kuli abashiileko amashiwi yandi?
I want bed and breakfast only	Ndeefwaya apaakulaala elyo na umwikulo
I want lunch included	Ndeefwaya icakulya cakasuba cipendelweko
Porter	Intumi
Please help with my bags	Mukwai ngafweniko ukusenda ifyoola
It's heavy	Naacifina
Please fetch me a taxi	Mfwaileeniko taxi

SHOPPING

At the…	Kuu…
Market	Maliketi
Shop	Ituuka
Grocers	Banamatuuka
Chemist	Umo bashita umuti
Gift shop	Ituuka lyabupe
I want one	Ndeefwaya cimo
Give me this/these, please	Mpeeni ici
How much is it?	Nishinga?
Money	Indalama
That's too expensive	Camutengo uukulu
Can you lower the price?	Bwesheniko umutengo?
Have you got anything cheaper?	Naamukwatako icinakile umutengo?

It's nice/beautiful	Ciisuma/naaciwama
I like it	Naacitemwa
I don't like it	Nshachitemwa
Yes, please	Ee, mukwai
No, thank you	Awe, mukwai
Do you sell…?	Mulashitisha…
Here's the money	Ishi mpiya
Have you got change for this?	Naamukwata change kuli ici?
Please can I have my change?	Mpeni change yandi mukwai?
I'll buy it	Naalaashita
How many?	Fili finga?
I don't have enough money	Nshikwete indalama ishingi
It's too big/small	Ciikulu/ciinoono saana
Do you have it in my size?	Naamukwata iciinganinga?
Do you have it in this colour?	Naamukwata lyamusango uyu?
I want a/some…	Ndeefwayako…
Can I try this/these on?	Kuti naeshamo ichi/ifi?
I need a receipt	Ndeefwaya lishiti

Sometimes you can swap things for goods, e.g. a t-shirt could be used as part payment towards a souvenir.

AT THE POST OFFICE

Where is the Post Office?	Yaba kwi Post Office?
How much is a stamp for…?	Nishinga stampa…?
I want to send this letter/ parcel to…	Ndeefwaya ukutuma ii kalata/ paselo kuli…
Five stamps for letters/ postcards to… please	Amastampa yasaano ayamakalata/amapostcard yaku…, mukwai

English	Bemba
Where can I post them?	Kuti naaposita kwi?
Please give me an airmail envelope	Mukwai mpeeni eyameelu enifulupu
Do you sell airmail writing paper?	Bushe mulashitisha amapeepala yakulembapo aya eyameelu?

IN A RESTAURANT/CAFÉ

English	Bemba
I want a table for… people	Ndeefwaya itebulo ilyabantu…
Near the window	Mupeepi ne windo
I want to eat…	Ndeefwaya ukulya…
I want to drink…	Ndeefwaya ukunwa…
Breakfast	Icakulya caluceelo
Lunch	Icakulya cakasuba
Dinner	Icakulya cacungulo-bushiku
Snack	Snaaki
What's the speciality?	Finshi ifiwemo ko?
What do you recommend?	Finshi mwingatiila efiwamiishe?
Knife	Umwele
Fork	Foloko
Spoon	Supuuni
Plate	Imbale
Cup	Kaapu
Glass	Ikalash
Dish	Akadishi
I've made a reservation	Niinsungishaumuputule
My name is…	Ishina lyandi nine…
That's not what I ordered	Ifyo teefyo naacishita
Dinner is ready	Icakulya cacungulo-ubushiku cateyanishiwa

Can I have some more of this, please?	Mpeeniko na fimbi ifyamusango-uyu mukwai?
Can I see the menu/wine list?	Kuti naamonako icipeepala mutantiikepo ifyakulya na umwangaashi mukwete?
I'd like to have a…	Ndeefwaya mumpeeleko…
What drinks do you have?	Fyakunwanshi mukwete?
Where can I get a drink?	Nikwi ninga sanga ifyakunwa?
Would you like tea or coffee?	Bushe uleefwaya tii nangu kofi?
I'll have a beer please	Mumpeeleko ubwalwa mukwai
One cup of coffee	Kaapu umo uwa kofi
Cheers!	Tunwe bwino!
Can I have some salt, please	Mpeeniko umucele
This is delicious	Fiisuma ifi
I don't want anything else	Nshileefwaya nangu ciimo
The bill, please	Mpeeniko billi mukwai

FOOD AND DRINK

Food	Ifyakulya
Coffee	Kofi
Tea	Tii
Beer	Ubwalwa
Water	Ameenshi
Beef	Inama yangombe
Pork	Inama yankumba
Chicken	Inkoko
Fish	Isabi
Maize	Inyanje
Tomato	Matimati

Okra	Umulembwe
Pumpkin leaves	Cibwabwa
Beans	Cilemba
Rice	Umupunga
Sweet potato	Ifyumbu
Onion	Kanyense
Salt	Umucele
Sugar	Shuka
Cold	Ukutalala
Hot	Ukukaba
Sweet	Ifyalowa
Spicy	Ifyanunkila

The staple food in Zambia is nshima, *made with mealie meal, served with relish and eaten with your hands.*

GETTING HELP

Help!	Ngafweniko!
Call the police	Iteeni baakapokola!
I need an ambulance	Ndeefwaya ambulanshi
I feel ill	Ndeumfwa ukubwala
I've been robbed	Baanjibila
I need a doctor	Ndeefwaya shinganga
My… hurts	Ndeumfwa… ubukali
Head	Umutwe
Stomach	Mumala
Arm	Ukuboko
Leg	Ukuulu

Back	Inuma
It hurts here	Cileekalipa apa
I can't sleep	Nshileelaala
I'm feeling worse	Nshileumfwa bwino
I'm feeling better	Ndeumfwa bwino
Take me to the…	Ntwaleeni ku…
Hospital	Cipataala
Doctor	Shingaga
Police	Baakapokola
I've lost my passport	Naalufya passport yandi
My money's been stolen	Indalama shandi naashiibwa
I left it in my room/on the bus	Nishiile muputule wandi/ muli saaca
Is there someone who can help me?	Bushe kuli uwingangafwako?
It's an emergency	Naacipamfya
We need help urgently	Tuleefwayako ubwafwilisho mukwangufyanya
Call the police/ambulance/ fire brigade	Iteeni baakapokola/ambulanshi/ abashimya umulilo
Where are you?	Uli kwi?
I'm at…	Ndi ku…
What's happened?	Cinshi cacitika?
There's been an accident/a fire	Kwaciba ubusanso/umulilo
It's serious	Naacibiipa nganshi

To call for help, dial 999 and state which sort of assistance you require.

DAYS, TIME AND WEATHER

Monday	Pali cimo
Tuesday	Pali cibili
Wednesday	Pali citatu
Thursday	Pali cine
Friday	Pali cisaano
Saturday	Pa cibelushi
Sunday	Pa mulungu
Today	Ileelo
Yesterday	Mailo
Tomorrow	Mailo
Last week	Umulungu wapwa
Last month	Umweshi wapwa
Last year	Umwaka wapwa
Next week	Umulungu uleisa
Next month	Umweshi uleisa
Next year	Umwaka uleisa
Morning	Uluceelo
Afternoon	Icungulo-kasuba
Evening	Icungulo-bushiku
Night	Ubushiku
See you tomorrow!	Tukamonana mailo!
See you on Friday!	Tukamonana pali cisaano!
Now	Nomba
Then	Elyo
Later	Paanuma
Before	Libe
After	Paanuma

What time is it?	Ninshitanshi ino?
It's… o'clock	Ninshita ya…

Zambia uses the twenty-four clock in telling the time, e.g. 6pm – 18:00 hours.

What's the weather like?	Bushe umwela uli shaani?
It's hot	Naakukaba
It's cold	Naakutalala
It's rainy	Ileeloka
It's windy	Umwela

NUMBERS AND MONEY

One	Cimo
Two	Fibili
Three	Fitatu
Four	Fine
Five	Fisaano
Six	Mutanda
Seven	Cine-lubali
Eight	Cine-konse-konse
Nine	Paabula
Ten	Ikumi

For higher numbers, use English.
The Zambian currency is Kwacha and Ngwee.

VERBS

To be	**Ukuba**
I am	Ndi
You (familiar/single) are	Uli
S/he is	Ali
We are	Tuli
You (polite/plural) are	Muli
They are	Bali

To have	**Ukukwata**
I have	Niinkwata
You (familiar/single) have	Naukwata
S/he has	Naakwata
We have	Naatukwata
You (polite/plural) have	Naamukwata
They have	Naabakwata

To want	**Ukuyfwaya**
I want	Ndeefwaya
You (familiar/single) want	Uleefwaya
S/he wants	Aleefwaya
We want	Tuleefwaya
You (polite/plural) want	Muleefwaya
They want	Baleefwaya

To like	**Ukutemwa**
I like	Naalitemwa
You (familiar/single) like	Walitemwa
S/he likes	Aalitemwa
We like	Twalitemwa
You (polite/plural) like	Mwalitemwa
They like	Baalitemwa

VERB LIST

To go	Ukuya
To come	Ukwisa
To eat	Ukulya
To drink	Ukunwa
To sleep	Ukulaala
To walk	Ukwenda
To buy	Ukushita
To see	Ukumona
To stay	Ukwikala
To stop	Ukuleka
To travel	Ukwende
To pay	Ukulipila
To choose	Ukusala
To help	Ukwafwa
To cook	Ukwipika
To rest	Ukutuusha
To feel	Ukuumfwa
To speak	Ukulanda
To give	Ukupeela
To ask	Ukwipusha

To know	Ukwishiba
To think	Ukutontonkanya
To be happy	Ukusansamuka

KAONDE

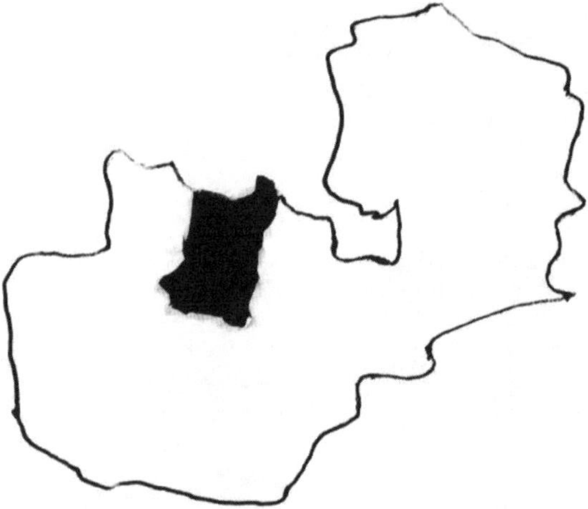

The Kaonde-speaking people of Zambia live mainly in the North-Western Province.

'Mukwenda mukunanga malubikilo kumusanza'
On travel it is visiting, returning it is home

GREETINGS AND FIRST WORDS

Hello	Mutende
How are you?	Mujibyepi?
I'm fine. And you?	Njitu bulongo. Kana nweba?
Fine, thank you	Njitu bulongo mwane
Good morning	Mwabuka byepi
Good afternoon	Kimabanga mwane
Good night	Kibufuku mwane
Goodbye	Shalaipo
See you!	Tusakumonañana!
Yes	Eee
No	Ine
Maybe	Kampe
Okay/fine	Kijitu/kyawama
Excuse me	Bandekeleko mambo mwane
Sorry	Kubulanda
Thank you very much	Na santa bingi
What's your name?	Wiñanyijizhina
My name is…	Jizhina jamine…
Pleased to meet you	Inasantapakukumana nenu
Please come in	Nasana twelai
Please sit down	Mwane ikalai panshi
Welcome	Mwaiyai
Please can you help me?	Napapata nkwasheko mwane?

Who?	Nanyi?
What?	Kika?
Where?	Kwepi?
When?	Kimyeka?
Why?	Mamboka?
Which?	Kyepi?
How?	Nanyi jishinda?

To show respect, preface the name of the person you are talking to with 'Ba', e.g. May – Ba Mary; Mr Phiri – Ba Phiri.

GENERAL CONVERSATION

Do you speak English?	Obewa wamba kizunguunyi?
I don't speak Kaonde	Amiwa kechi ñgamba kikaonde
I speak a little Kaonde	Ñgamba kikaonde pacheche
I am learning Kaonde	Amiwa mbena kufunda kikaonde
Sorry, I don't understand	Kena umvwane bwezhaipo
Please repeat that	Bweezhaipo nasansapo
Please speak slowly	Nasansapo nwambenga bichebiche
What is this?	Kika kye?
How do you say… in Kaonde?	Mwamba byepi… mu kikaonde?
How do you say… in English?	Mwamba byepi… mukizungu?
Did I pronounce it right?	Bushe nakwikilumbulula bulongonyi?
Do you understand me?	Ubena kunumvwanyi?
This is my…	Abibyami
Wife	Mukazhi

Husband	Mulume
Son	Mwana wamulume
Daughter	Mwana wamukazhi
Sister	Nyenga
Brother	Yaya
Friend	Mukwetu
Family	Balongo
I work as a…	Ñingila bu…
I am… years old	Njina myaka yafikala ku…
Are you married?	Mwasongolwa?
I am married	Nasongolwa
I am not married	Kenasongolwane
How many children do you have?	Ujina baana banga?
I don't have any children	Kenji po na baana ne
I have… children	Njina… baana
I am on holiday	Njipa kukokoloka
I am working here	Mbena kwingila pano
I live here	Ngikala pano
Where do you come from?	Mufumapi?
I am from…	Nafuma…
Can I take a photo?	Kana nkpowe?
Where is the toilet?	Kyolonyi kijipi?
Entrance	Kibeelo
Exit	Mwakulupukila
Ladies	Bana bakazhi
Gentlemen	Babalume
Me	Amiwa
You	Obewa
She	Womukazhi
He	Wamulume

We	Atweba
They	Abo
I feel cold/hot	Naumvwa mashika/kukaba
I feel tired	Naumvwa kukoka
I am hungry and thirsty	Nafwanzala nekilaka
I like it here	Nekutemwa bingi kuno
Mr	Ba
Mrs	Bamuka
Miss	Wamukazhi wabula kusongolwa
See you later	Tukamonañana kimye kikwabo
See you tomorrow	Tukamonañana kesha
Why?	Mambo ka?
Because…	Mambo…
I don't understand	Kenaumvwane
I don't know	Kenayukana
I think…	Nalanguluka…
I want…	Nasaka…
I don't want…	Kembena kusakane…
I like…	Natemwa…
I don't like…	Kenatemwa ne…

GETTING AROUND

Excuse me, where is…?	Bankwashekomwane, kweepi kuji…?
Where are the…?	Kweepi kuji…
Shops	Mashitolo
Restaurants	Azubo yakujilamo
Night clubs	Kimvwange kya bufuku?

Where is the…?	Kweepi kuji…?
Lake	Kizhiba
River	Mukola
Village	Muzhi
Game park	Jisa kajaba nyama
Post Office	Positi ofweshi
Bank	Banki
Bureau de Change	Kobapimpwila mali amukyalo kingi
Museum	Mphunzha koba mwesha bintu
Church	Kipwilo
Bus stop	Kwimena masakya
Train station	Kiteshenyi kya shitima
Airport	Kibanza kya ndeke
Where is this?	Nangwa ijipi?
Can I walk there?	Nakonsha kwenda kokwa?
Do you have a map?	Ujina mapunyi?
Can you show me?	Wakonsha kumwee shanyi?
To the…	Ku…
Left	Kipiko
Right	Kilujo
Straight ahead	Kulungama palutwe
Where are you going?	Ubena kuyapi?
I am going to…	Mbena kuya ku…
Is this the way to…?	Ajejojishinda ja kunanga…?
I want to travel by…	Mbena kusakakuyana…
Bicycle	Nkinga
Motorbike	Kitukutuku
Boat	Bwato
Horse	Mbili

Vehicle (general)	Motoka
How much does the journey cost?	Malianga lwendo lonse?
How long will it take?	Bimyebinga pa kubamba mufike?
Can I buy a ticket?	Nakousha kupota jichiki ehi nyi?
Where's the bus/train/plane/ boat for…?	Iji kwepi sakya/shitima/ndeke/ bwato bwa…?
How can I go there?	Nakonsha kuya kokwa byepi?
I want to see the…	Nasakakumona…
Is there a driver?	Apajiko mwendeshi nyi?
Can I go today?	Nakousha kuya lelo nyi?
Is there an entrance fee?	Poajimali akutwelela pakibelonyi?
What are the opening hours?	Bashinkula bimyeka?
It's open from… to…	Bashinkula ku tatula… nekufika..
Street/road	Mukwakwa/jishinda
A little bit	Pachechetu
A lot	Vula byavula
Quickly	Bukiji
Slowly	Bichebiche
What's the best way to…?	Jepi jishimda jawama jaku…?
Should I take a taxi?	Ngyena takishi?
It's near the …	Kwipina…
Cross the road	Abukamukwakwa
Go past the…	Pitakunangwa…
It's near here	Pepitu napano
It's far from here	Kwalepa kufuma napano
It's too far to walk	Palepa bingi kwenda namaulu
It's ten minutes by foot	Maminetishi jikumi kwendana maulu

It's five minutes by car	Namotoka pa taya maminetishi atanu
Do I need my passport?	Kana kikebewa pasipotinyi?

PUBLIC TRANSPORT

Is this the right bus for…?	Ayiyoine sakya ya…?
Where's the nearest bus stop?	Paipipisha pemena sakya pepi?
How much is the fare?	Inga ya kukanjijila?
I'm going to…	Mbena kuya ku…
Where can I drop off?	Nakonsha kwikiji la pepi?
Which bus/train can I take to..?	Sakya ka/shitima ka yonakonsha kuya nayo ku…?
Can I have my change?	Bampe mali ami ashalako?
Please stop here	Nasansapomwane bemane ponkapano

CARS

I want to hire a car	Nasaka kuteula ka motoka
Where's the best place to rent a car?	Mpunzha yawama koba sonkela tumyotoka iji kwepi?
I want a small/large vehicle	Nasaka motoka icheche/yabaya
I want it today/tomorrow	Neiksaka lelo/kesha
How much do you charge?	Mulipijisha inga?
Fill it up please	Nasansapo yuyzhai
The tyre's flat	Mupila wasabika
It's broken down	Yaonaika
Can you fix it?	Wakonsha kulungishanyi?

Is there a garage/mechanic near here?	Kujiko mwakulungishisha pepi nyi?
When will it be ready?	Isa kupwa kimyeka?
Can you do it now?	Wakonsha kuba katataka?

GAME VIEWING

We want to go somewhere on Friday	Tubena kukeba kuyapo kumo pakitanu
There'll be two of us	Tukekala atweba babiji
Is it worth seeing?	Kyawama kumonanyi?
Is it suitable for children?	Kyawamatu ne kubaananyi?
How much does it cost?	Kipotwa inga?
What does the price include?	Mumu tengo mwatwe laineka?
What time will we leave?	Tusa kuya kimyeka?
What time will we get back?	Tusakubwela kimyeka?
Is lunch included?	Nekajakapachaile kaji monkanyi?
Where do I buy a ticket?	Nsakupota kweepi jichi kichi?
Buffalo	Mboo
Crocodile	Kiwele
Elephant	Nzovu
Giraffe	Njabuluba
Hippopotamus	Kyovwemulume
Lion	Bokwe
Monkey	Kolwe
Rhinoceros	Kipembele
Snake	Mulolo
Zebra	Kilangwa

AT THE HOTEL

I want a good hotel	Mbena kusaka yawama hotela
Do you have a room available?	Mujina kipinda kyaikalatunyi?
I want a room for… people	Nasakamukipinda mwabantu..
With a nice view	Nekimwekelo kyawama
For one night/two nights/ one week	Kyabufuku bumo/bubi ji/ mulungu umo
I've made a reservation	Neinengezha kala bya
My name is…	Jizhina jami ne…
How much is a room?	Inga papinda?
Is breakfast included?	Kajo kalukelo bek abikakonyi?
Is it air conditioned?	Kitukulwanamwela?
You are in room number…	Muji mukipinda kya nambalaka..
Please give me a wake-up call at	Nasansapo mukambushe pona kimye kya…
Is there a restaurant here?	Kujimwa kujila kunonyi?
Is there a…	Kujina nangwa…
Swimming pool	Mwakowela
Gym	Nzubo mwakukaila
Hairdressers	Mwakuso kela nsuki
Gift shop	Shitolo wabyabupe
Night club	Mwakutomena malwa bufuku
Business centre	Mpunzha yamingilo
Room service	Kipinda kyamingilo
Please bring… to my room	Mwane leta… kukipinda kyami
Please bring my luggage	Mwane ndetelaiko kipe kyami
Are there any messages for me?	Kujipo mawi ami nyi?
I want bed and breakfast only	Mbena kusaka mwanyane kajokalukelo kyapwa

I want lunch included	Nasaka chaile ikaleponka
Porter	Kyola boyi
Please help with my bags	Mwane nkwashaiko nabyloa byami
It's heavy	Kyanema
Please fetch me a taxi	Mwane kebelaiko takishi

SHOPPING

At the…	Pa…
Market	Kisankanyi
Shop	Shitolo
Grocers	Mitola
Chemist	Mutanwa michi
Gift shop	Shitolo wabupe
I want one	Nasaka kimo
Give me this/these, please	Mwane, mpai kikye/bimye
How much is it?	Inga kikye?
That's too expensive	Akyo kyabaisha mutengo
Can you lower the price?	Kemwakonsha kubwezha konenyi?
Have you got anything cheaper?	Mujipona byapela?
It's nice/beautiful	Kya wama/kumoneka buya
I like it	Nekitemwa
I don't like it	Kenekitemwane
Yes, please	Ee, mwane
No, thank you	Ine nasanta
Do you sell…?	Mupoteshanyi…?
Here's the money	Mali ano

Have you got change for this?	Mujipolupi mpumu kikyenyi?
Please can I have my change?	Mwane mali ami ashalapo?
I'll buy it	Nsakukapota
How many?	Binga?
I don't have enough money	Kenjinamali avulane
It's too big/small	Kyabaishatu/kyakepeshatu
Do you have it in my size?	Uji ponakyamunsaishi yaminyi?
Do you have it in this colour?	Ujiponakyo muyiwemu tu ndunyi?
I want a/some…	Nasakapo kimo/bimo…
Can I try this/these on?	Nakonsha kweseka kikye/bibye?
I need a receipt	Nasaka kapepala

Sometimes you can swap things for goods, e.g. a t-shirt could be used as part payment towards a souvenir.

AT THE POST OFFICE

Where is the Post Office?	Posti ofweshi wepi?
How much is a stamp for…?	Inga shita mpu wa…?
I want to send this letter/ parcel to…	Nasa ka kutuma nkala ta…
Five stamps for letters/ postcards to… please	Atano mashitampu amakalata/ atanu pa…
Where can I post them?	Nakonsha kutumi namwepi?
Please give me an airmail envelope	Mwane mpai enivulupo wa kutuma bya mumwela
Do you sell airmail writing paper?	Kananyi mupotesha mapepala akulembapo makalata?

IN A RESTAURANT/CAFÉ

I want a table for… people	Nasaka tebulu wabantu…
Near the window	Pepina kapeze
I want to eat…	Nasak kuja…
I want to drink…	Nasaka kutoma…
Breakfast	Kaja kalukelu
Lunch	Kajo kapachaile
Dinner	Kajo kamabanga
Snack	Tukajo twapela
What's the speciality?	Kikakya wamisha?
What do you recommend?	Mwaamba ambaka?
Knife	Mupenyi
Fork	Foloko
Spoon	Mujisho
Plate	Muchiba
Cup	Nkomoki
Glass	Galashi
Dish	Dishi
I've made a reservation	Nanengezha byakuteula
My name is…	Jishina jamine…
That's not what I ordered	Kebyonakebelebyone
Dinner is ready	Kajo kapya
Can I have some more of this, please?	Bampeponebikwa bo mwane?
Can I see the menu/wine list?	Nakonshakumona mutanghi wa kajo/binyu?
I'd like to have a…	Nafwainwa kwikala na…
What drinks do you have?	Nasaka byakutoma?

Where can I get a drink?	Kwepi kona konsha kutana byakutoma?
Would you like tea or coffee?	Watemwa makabe achi nyi/kofi?
I'll have a beer please	Nsakutomapo kamalwa kemo nwane
One cup of coffee	Nikomo ki wakofi
Cheers!	Nsekelai!
Can I have some salt, please	Mpekoi mukele mwane
This is delicious	Bino bya wama kukilapo
I don't want anything else	Kembena kusaka ne bintu bikwabe
The bill, please	Nkongole mwane

FOOD AND DRINK

Food	Kajo
Coffee	Kofi
Tea	Makabe
Beer	Malwa
Water	Mema
Beef	Nyama
Pork	Nkumba
Chicken	Nzaio
Fish	Masabi
Maize	Mataba
Tomato	Matemate
Okra	Mulembwe
Pumpkin leaves	Bishu
Beans	Nkunde
Rice	Mupunga

Sweet potato	Ntamba
Onion	Kanyeze
Salt	Mukele
Sugar	Sukale
Cold	Kutalala
Hot	Kukuba
Sweet	Kutobala
Spicy	Binukila byamumanyi

The staple food in Zambia is nshima, *made with mealie meal, served with relish and eaten with your hands.*

GETTING HELP

Help!	Bukwasho!
Call the police	Itakapokola!
I need an ambulance	Mbenakusa motoka utwalababeela
I feel ill	Naumvwa kubeela
I've been robbed	Bandajila
I need a doctor	Mbena kusaka dokotala
My… hurts	Ami… akola
Head	Mutwe
Stomach	Kifu
Arm	Kuboko
Leg	Kuulu
Back	Nyuma
It hurts here	Kibena kukolela pape
I can't sleep	Kenakonshakulalane

I'm feeling worse	Mbena kumvisha kyakil amo
I'm feeling better	Mbena ku mvwa kobu longo
Take me to the…	Ntwalaiku…
Hospital	Kipatela
Doctor	Dokotala
Police	Polishi
I've lost my passport	Naela pasowami
My money's been stolen	Mali amibaiba
I left it in my room/on the bus	Nashile mu kipinda/musakya
Is there someone who can help me?	Pajipo wakonshaku nkwasha aminyi?
It's an emergency	Kyakubazhimukila
We need help urgently	Twena kukeba bukwasho katataka
Call the police/ambulance/ fire brigade	Ita kapokola/ambulashi/ motoka izhima mujilo
Where are you?	Uji kwepi?
I'm at…	Njiku pa…
What's happened?	Kika kyamwekana?
There's been an accident	Kujimapuso
It's serious	Kya tamabingi

To call for help, dial 999 and state which sort of assistance you require.

DAYS, TIME AND WEATHER

Monday	Pakimo
Tuesday	Pakibiji
Wednesday	Pakisatu
Thursday	Pakina
Friday	Pakitanu
Saturday	Pakibelushi
Sunday	Pamulungu
Today	Lelo
Yesterday	Kesha
Tomorrow	Kesha
Last week	Mulungu wapwa
Last month	Ñondo wapwa
Last year	Mwaka wapwa
Next week	Mulungu wiya
Next month	Ñondo wiya
Next year	Mwaka wiya
Morning	Lukelo
Afternoon	Mute
Evening	Mabanga
Night	Bufuku
See you tomorrow!	Tukamonañana kesha!
See you on Friday!	Tukamonañana pakitanu!
Now	Luno
Then	Akya kimye
Later	Katataka
Before	Saka
After	Kupwisha popa

What time is it?	Kimye kyafika bypei?
It's… o'clock	Biji… koloko

Zambia uses the twenty-four clock in telling the time, e.g. 6pm – 18:00 hours.

What's the weather like?	Mwela ujibyepi?
It's hot	Kwauba kyuya
It's cold	Kwatalala
It's rainy	Kujimvula
It's windy	Kujimwela

NUMBERS AND MONEY

One	Kamo
Two	Tubiji
Three	Tusatu
Four	Tuna
Five	Tutanu
Six	Tutanu na kamo
Seven	Tutanu na tubiji
Eight	Tutanu na tusatu
Nine	Tutanu na tuna
Ten	Jikumi

For higher numbers, use English.
The Zambian currency is Kwacha and Ngwee.

VERBS

To be	
I am	Amu
You (familiar/single) are	Mu
S/he is	U (wamukazhi/wamulume)
We are	Tubena
You (polite/plural) are	Mubena
They are	Babena

To have	
I have	Njina
You (familiar/single) have	Muji
S/he has	Uji wamukazhi/wamulume
We have	Tujina
You (polite/plural) have	Muji
They have	Baji

To want	**Kusaka**
I want	Nasaka
You (familiar/single) want	Wasaka
S/he wants	Wasaka wamukazhi/wamulume
We want	Twasaka
You (polite/plural) want	Mwasaka
They want	Basaka

To like	**Kutemwa**
I like	Natemwa
You (familiar/single) like	Watemwa
S/he likes	Watemwa (wamukazhi/ wamuleme)
We like	Twatemwa
You (polite/plural) like	Mwatemwa
They like	Batema

VERB LIST

To go	Kuya
To come	Kwiiya
To eat	Kuja
To drink	Kutooma
To sleep	Kulaala
To walk	Kweenda
To buy	Kupoota
To see	Kumona
To stay	Kwikala
To stop	Kwimana
To travel	Kkwenda
To pay	Kulipila
To choose	Kusala
To help	Kukwasha
To cook	Kuteeka
To rest	Kutusha
To feel	Kumvwa
To speak	Kwamba
To give	Kupana

To ask	Kwipuzha
To know	Kuyuka
To think	Kulanguluka
To be happy	Kusangalala

LOZI

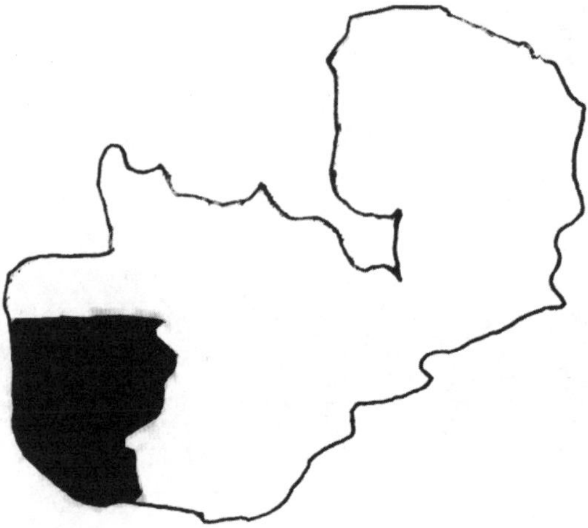

The Lozi-speaking people of Zambia live mainly in the Western Province.

'Nde alyamui ahatandwa peunja yojya muwa'
When a lion eats a bad person and it is not killed, tomorrow it will eat a good person

GREETINGS AND FIRST WORDS

Hello	Sha
How are you?	Mucwani
I'm fine. And you?	Napila. Mina bo?
Fine, thank you	Kihande nitumezi
Good morning	Muzuhile cwani
Good afternoon	Mutozi
Good night	Mulobale hande
Goodbye	Musiyale hande
See you!	Lukabonana!
Yes	Eeni
No	Batili
Maybe	Mwendi
Okay/fine	Kulukile/kihona
Excuse me	Amuniswalele
Sorry	Niswabile
Thank you very much	Nitumezi hahulu
What's your name?	Libizo lamina kimina bomani?
My name is…	Libizo laka kina…
Pleased to meet you	Nitumezi alukopani
Please come in	Amuine
Please sit down	Ina afasi
Welcome	Mwamuhezwi

Please can you help me?	Nikupatuso?
Who?	Ufi?
What?	Kini?
Where?	Kai?
When?	Lili?
Why?	Kabakalani?
Which?	Sifi?
How?	Cwani?

To show respect, preface the name of the person you are talking to with 'Ba', e.g. May – Ba Mary; Mr Phiri – Ba Phiri.

GENERAL CONVERSATION

Do you speak English?	Wabulela Sikuwa?
I don't speak Lozi	Anibuleli Silozi?
I speak a little Lozi	Niziba hanyinyani Silozi
I am learning Lozi	Naituta Silozi
Sorry, I don't understand	Muniswalele aniutwi
Please repeat that	Hamu kutele
Please speak slowly	Hamubulele kabunya
What is this?	Kini se?
How do you say… in Lozi?	Mubulela cwani… mwa Silozi?
How do you say… in English?	Mubulela cwani… mwa Sikuwa?
Did I pronounce it right?	Nibulezi hande?
Do you understand me?	Muni utwisisize nji?
This is my…	Yoki…
Wife	Musali yanyezwi
Husband	Muuna yanyezi
Son	Mwana wa mushimani

Daughter	Mwana wa musizana
Sister	Kezeli wamusali
Brother	Kezeli wamuuna
Friend	Mulikani
Family	Lubasi
I work as a…	Nibeleka inge…
I am… years old	Ninani lilimo…
Are you married?	Unyezwi?
I am married	Ninyezwi
I am not married	Anisikanyalwa
How many children do you have?	Unani bana babakai?
I don't have any children	Anina mwana
I have… children	Ninani bana baba…
I am on holiday	Ninzi fa pumulo
I am working here	Nibeleka kwanu
I live here	Nipila kwanu
Where do you come from?	Muzwa kai?
I am from…	Nizwa kwa…
Can I take a photo?	Anikoni kuunga siswaniso?
Where is the toilet?	Simbuzi sikai?
Entrance	Makenelo
Exit	Munyako
Ladies	Boma
Gentlemen	Bondate
Me	Na
You	Mina
She	Yena
He	Yena
We	Luna
They	Bona

I feel cold/hot	Niutwa kubata/kuchisa
I feel tired	Niutwa kukatala
I am hungry and thirsty	Niutwa tala nilinyolwa
I like it here	Nalata kwanu
Mr	Munali
Mrs	Mufumahali
Miss	Bo
See you later	Lukabonana ape
See you tomorrow	Lukabonana kamuso
Why?	Kabakalani?
Because…	Bakenisa…
I don't understand	Aniutwisisi
I don't know	Anizibi
I think…	Ninahana…
I want…	Nibata…
I don't want…	Anilati…
I like…	Nilata…
I don't like…	Anilati…

GETTING AROUND

Excuse me, where is…?	Nabuza sha, …ikai?
Where are the…	Kikai…
Shops	Lintolo
Restaurants	Koku lekiswa lico
Night clubs	Kwa manwelo abushi
Where is the…?	Kikai…
Lake	Lisa
River	Nuka
Village	Munzi

Game park	Kokufumane lifolofolo
Post Office	Ofisi ya poso
Bank	Kwa panga
Bureau de Change	Lokucinjezwa mali
Museum	Kokufumanwa zakale
Church	Kwa keleke
Bus stop	Kokupahamelwa libasi
Train station	Kokupahamelwa sitima
Airport	Libala lafulai
Where is this?	Ikai?
Can I walk there?	Nakonakufita kwateni ka mautu nji?
Do you have a map?	Munani mapu?
Can you show me?	Mwakona kunisupeza kwateni?
To the…	Kwa…
Left	Nzohoto
Right	Kwasilyo
Straight ahead	Kuzwelapili
Where are you going?	Muyakai?
I am going to…	Niya kwa…
Is this the way to…?	Kana ye kiyona nzila yeya kwa...?
I want to travel by…	Nibata kuzamaya ka…
Bicycle	Njinga
Motorbike	Mutututu
Boat	Sisepe
Horse	Pizi
Vehicle (general)	Mota
How much does the journey cost?	Musipili ulifwa bukai?
How long will it take?	Utanga nako yekuma kai?
Can I buy a ticket?	Nakonakuleka tikiti nji?

Where's the bus/train/ plane/boat for...?	Mbasi ikai/sitima sikai/ fulai/sisepe sesi ya kwa...?
How can I go there?	Nikona kufita cwani kwateni?
I want to see the...	Nibata ku bona...
Is there a driver?	Kunani dilaiba?
Can I go today?	Nakona kuya kacenu?
Is there an entrance fee?	Balifisa kukena nji?
What are the opening hours?	Bakala ku beleka nakomani?
It's open from... to...	Bakwalula ka... kuisa ka...
Street/road	Mukwakwa
A little bit	Hanyinyani fela
A lot	Hahulu
Quickly	Kapili
Slowly	Kabunya
What's the best way to...?	Kiifi nzila kuya kwa...?
Should I take a taxi?	Nikwele mota nji?
It's near the ...	Kifa kaufi ni...
Cross the road	Mutule mukwakwa
Go past the...	Kufite lela...
It's near here	Mufitelele
It's far from here	Kikwahule
It's too far to walk	Kikwa hule kamautu
It's ten minutes by foot	Ki mizuzu yelishumi ka mautu
It's five minutes by car	Ki mizuzu yeketalizoho ka mota
Do I need my passport?	Natokwa pasipoti yaka nji?

PUBLIC TRANSPORT

Is this the right bus for...?	Kana bus ye iya kwa...?
Where's the nearest bus stop?	Kikai koku kwelelwa?

How much is the fare?	Libukai litifo?
I'm going to…	Niyakwa…
Where can I drop off?	Niswanela kutulukela kai?
Which bus/train can I take to..?	Basi/sitima ya kwa… ki ifi?
Can I have my change?	Amunife change yaka?
Please stop here	Amuyeme onafa

CARS

I want to hire a car	Nibata kubukina mota
Where's the best place to rent a car?	Kikai konikona kufumana mota yakuitusisa?
I want a small/large vehicle	Nibata mota yenyinyani/yetuna
I want it today/tomorrow	Niibata kachenu/kamuso
How much do you charge?	Mulifisa bukai?
Fill it up please	Amubeye mwateni mafula
The tyre's flat	Taya ifopile
It's broken down	Mota injombile
Can you fix it?	Mwakona kuilukisa?
Is there a garage/mechanic near here?	Kikai koku fumaneha galeiji/makanika kwanu?
When will it be ready?	Itakonda lili?
Can you do it now?	Mwakona kulukisa onafa?

GAME VIEWING

We want to go somewhere on Friday	Lubata kuyopota labufaifi
There'll be two of us	Lutaba bababeli
Is it worth seeing?	Kana kwatabisa kubuha?
Is it suitable for children?	Kana kwaswanela banana?

How much does it cost?	Kibukai tifo?
What does the price include?	Kilikamani zebatahala?
What time will we leave?	Lufunduka nako mani ka?
What time will we get back?	Lukuta nako mani?
Is lunch included?	Niza kuca musihali?
Where do I buy a ticket?	Kikai kubalekisa matikiti?
Buffalo	Nali
Crocodile	Kwena
Elephant	Tou
Giraffe	Tutwa
Hippopotamus	Kubu
Lion	Tau
Monkey	Njoko
Rhinoceros	Sukulu
Snake	Noha
Zebra	Pizi

AT THE HOTEL

I want a good hotel	Nibata hotela yende
Do you have a room available?	Sibaka siteni?
I want a room for… people	Nibata musiyo wabatu baba…
With a nice view	Apono yende
For one night/two nights/	Masihu amabeli/sunda ilinwi
I've made a reservation	Nibulukile sibaka
My name is…	Libizo laka kina…
How much is a room?	Kibukai musiyo ulimunwi?
Is breakfast included?	Kunani ni mukushuko ukopanyizwe nji?
Is it air conditioned?	Mushini wamoya obata?

You are in room number…	Musiyo wamina ki nombolo…
Please give me a wake-up call at	Nge munizuse ka… hours
Is there a restaurant here?	Kikai kokulekiswa lico?
Is there a…	Kunani…
Swimming pool	Kandumbi
Gym	Kwakubapalela
Hairdressers	Kwakulukiseza milili
Gift shop	Sintolo sa limpo
Night club	Kwaku tonela busihu-nilipina
Business centre	Kwa malikisezo
Room service	Sebelezo ya mwa musiyo
Please bring… to my room	Nakupa munitiseze.. kwa musiyo wake
Please bring my luggage	Nikupa kunitiseza libyana zaka
Are there any messages for me?	Akunaze lizibiso zaka?
I want bed and breakfast only	Nibata mumbeta mukushuko
I want lunch included	Nibata saku ca samusihali
Porter	Mulwali
Please help with my bags	Amunituse kunilwalisa mikotana
It's heavy	Ibukiti
Please fetch me a taxi	Amuni batele takisi

SHOPPING

At the…	Kwa…
Market	Musika
Shop	Sintolo
Grocers	Lintolo
Chemist	Sintolo sa milyani
Gift shop	Sintolo sa limpo

I want one	Nibata ilinwi
Give me this/these, please	Amunife ze
How much is it?	Kibukai?
That's too expensive	Siatula hahalu
Can you lower the price?	Amunikutiseze kwa teko?
Have you got anything cheaper?	Amuna sesicipile?
It's nice/beautiful	Kisesinde
I like it	Na silata
I don't like it	Anisilati
Yes, please	Eni, sha
No, thank you	Batili niitumezi
Do you sell…?	Mwa lekisa…?
Here's the money	Kia mali
Have you got change for this?	Mwakona kunicinceza?
Please can I have my change?	Nibata cinci yaka?
I'll buy it	Nita ileka
How many?	Zekai?
I don't have enough money	Hanina mali alikana
It's too big/small	Kisesituna/kikaka inyani hahulu
Do you have it in my size?	Size yaka iteni nji?
Do you have it in this colour?	Munani mubala wo nji?
I want a/some…	Nibata…
Can I try this/these on?	Nakona kuitikanyeza?
I need a receipt	Nibata lisiiti

Sometimes you can swap things for goods, e.g. a t-shirt could be used as part payment towards a souvenir.

AT THE POST OFFICE

Where is the Post Office?	Ofisi ya poso ikai?
How much is a stamp for…?	Kibukai sitempe…?
I want to send this letter/ parcel to…	Nibata kulumeleza linolo/ siputela…
Five stamps for letters/ postcards to… please	Nibata litempe a faifi/ lipositikadi sha…
Where can I post them?	Ni kapositela kai
Please give me an airmail envelope	Amunife kwateni ingilopu ya eyamailu
Do you sell airmail writing paper?	Mwalekisa mapampili e eyamailu akunolela?

IN A RESTAURANT/CAFÉ

I want a table for… people	Nibata tafule yabutu baba…
Near the window	Fakaufi niwindo
I want to eat…	Nibata kuca…
I want to drink…	Nibata kunwa…
Breakfast	Mukushuko
Lunch	Sico samusihali
Dinner	Sico samanzibwana
Snack	Nibata nisakucisa
What's the speciality?	Kisifi sesi nde?
What do you recommend?	Kisifi se muselumba?
Knife	Tipa
Fork	Tabisa
Spoon	Luswana

Plate	Mukeke
Cup	Komoki
Glass	Tambula
Dish	Musulo
I've made a reservation	Munibulukele
My name is…	Libizo laka kina…
That's not what I ordered	Anisika bata zeo batili
Dinner is ready	Lico lilukile
Can I have some more of this, please?	Mwakoma kunifa zonaze hape sha?
Can I see the menu/wine list?	Amuni supeze fokunozwi litifo/za lico?
I'd like to have a…	Amunife kwateni…
What drinks do you have?	Ki lifi zakunwa zemunani zona mani aliteni?
Where can I get a drink?	Kikai konikona kuleka zakunwa?
Would you like tea or coffee?	Mubata tii kapa kofi?
I'll have a beer please	Nibata bucwala sha
One cup of coffee	Komoki ilinwi ya kofi
Cheers!	Eheee!
Can I have some salt, please	Nibata kwa lizwai
This is delicious	Kisesinde sico se
I don't want anything else	Anibati sisili
The bill, please	Nilifa bukai

FOOD AND DRINK

Food	Lico
Coffee	Kofi
Tea	Tii

Beer	Bucwala
Water	Mezi
Beef	Nama ya komu
Pork	Nama ya kulube
Chicken	Kuhu
Fish	Litapi
Maize	Mbonyi
Tomato	Matamankisi
Okra	Delele
Pumpkin leaves	Mangambwa
Beans	Manawa
Rice	Raisi
Sweet potato	Ngulu
Onion	Nyanisi
Salt	Lizwai
Sugar	Swikili
Cold	Kwabata
Hot	Kwacisa
Sweet	Munati
Spicy	Munuhko waze beiwa mwa lico

The staple food in Zambia is nshima, *made with mealie meal, served with relish and eaten with your hands.*

GETTING HELP

Help!	Tuso!
Call the police	Amuibize mapokola
I need an ambulance	Amubize ambulasi
I feel ill	Niikutwa kukula

I've been robbed	Bani uzwelize
I need a doctor	Nibata dokota
My… hurts	Ni utwa butuku…
Head	Toho
Stomach	Mwamba
Arm	Lizoho
Leg	Lihutu
Back	Mukokoto
It hurts here	Ni utwa butuku fa
I can't sleep	Anikoni kulobala
I'm feeling worse	Ni utwa butuka hahulu
I'm feeling better	Ni ikutwa hande
Take me to the…	Amuniise kwa…
Hospital	Sipatela
Doctor	Dokota
Police	Mapokola
I've lost my passport	Ni latile pasipoti yaka
My money's been stolen	Mali aka auzwizwe
I left it in my room/on the bus	Ni isile mwa musiyo waka/bus
Is there someone who can help me?	Kimani yakona kutusa?
It's an emergency	Yetokwahala kabubebe
We need help urgently	Lubata tuso kakuakufa
Call the police/ambulance/ fire brigade	Amubize mapokola/basipatela/ batimi bamulilo
Where are you?	Mukai?
I'm at…	Nikwa…
What's happened?	Kuezahalile ni?
There's been an accident/a fire	Likolofalo/kunani kozi
It's serious	Kibutata

To call for help, dial 999 and state which sort of assistance you require.

DAYS, TIME AND WEATHER

Monday	Lamubulo
Tuesday	Labubeli
Wednesday	Labulalu
Thursday	Labune
Friday	Labufaifi
Saturday	Lapelekelo
Sunday	Lasunda
Today	Kacenu
Yesterday	Mabani
Tomorrow	Kamuso
Last week	Sunda yefelile
Last month	Kweli yefelile
Last year	Nohola
Next week	Sunda yetaha
Next month	Kweli yetaha
Next year	Isaho
Morning	Kakusasani
Afternoon	Musihali
Evening	Manibwana
Night	Busihu
See you tomorrow!	Lukabonana kamuso!
See you on Friday!	Lukabonana labufaifi!
Now	Onafa
Then	Ape
Later	Samulaho

Before	Pili
After	Hasamulaho
What time is it?	Kinako mani?
It's… o'clock	Ki… kiloko

Zambia uses the twenty-four clock in telling the time, e.g. 6pm – 18:00 hours.

What's the weather like?	Kuzuhile cwani kacenu?
It's hot	Kwacisa
It's cold	Kwabata
It's rainy	Kimulupi
It's windy	Kilamoya

NUMBERS AND MONEY

One	Kalikanwi
Two	Totubeli
Three	Totulalu
Four	Totune
Five	Totuketalizoho
Six	Totuketalizoho ni kalikamwi
Seven	Totuketalizoho ni totubeli
Eight	Totuketalizoho ni totulalu
Nine	Totuketalizoho ni totune
Ten	Lishumi

For higher numbers, use English.
The Zambian currency is Kwacha and Ngwee.

VERBS

To be	**Kuba**
I am	Na
You (familiar/single) are	Wena
S/he is	Wa
We are	Lwa
You (polite/plural) are	Mina
They are	Ba
To have	**Kuba**
I have	Ninani
You (familiar/single) have	Unani
S/he has	Unaani
We have	Lunani
You (polite/plural) have	Munani
They have	Banani
To want	**Kubata**
I want	Nibata
You (familiar/single) want	Wabata
S/he wants	Ubata
We want	Lubata
You (polite/plural) want	Mubata
They want	Babata

To like	**Kulata**
I like	Nalata
You (familiar/single) like	Walata
S/he likes	Waalata
We like	Lwalata
You (polite/plural) like	Mulata
They like	Balata

VERB LIST

To go	Kuya
To come	Kutaha
To eat	Kuca
To drink	Kunwa
To sleep	Kulobala
To walk	Kuzamaya
To buy	Kuleka
To see	Kubona
To stay	Kuina
To stop	Kutuhela
To travel	Kuzamaya
To pay	Kulifa
To choose	Kuketa
To help	Kutusa
To cook	Kwapeha
To rest	Kupumula
To feel	Kutwa
To speak	Kubulela
To give	Kufa
To ask	Kubuza

To know	Kuziba
To think	Kunahana
To be happy	Kutaba

LUNDA

The Lunda-speaking people of Zambia live mainly in the North-Western Province.

'Wakenga Menzhi Wadi Kujahanga Nswaha'
One who loves water will not break the calabash

GREETINGS AND FIRST WORDS

Hello	Halo
How are you?	Munahandi mwane?
I'm fine. And you?	Nidi cha chi wahi. Kwizi eyi?
Fine, thank you	Cha chi wahi, tunasakilili
Good morning	Munahandi mwane
Good afternoon	Munahandi mwane
Good night	Mukamami chachiwahi
Goodbye	Shalenuhu
See you!	Tuualimona!
Yes	Eng'a
No	Nehi
Maybe	Hadaha
Okay/fine	Ena chachiwahi
Excuse me	N'ganakenenuku
Sorry	Sole
Thank you very much	Tunasakilili nankashi
What's your name?	Ijina deyi yeyinyi?
My name is…	Injina dami yami…
Pleased to meet you	Natiyi muzangalu hakudiwana
Please come in	Mwani ungilenu
Please sit down	Wa ni ashakami
Welcome	Shikenu mwane
Please can you help me?	Nkwashenuku mwane?

Who?	Hinyi?
What?	Chika?
Where?	Kudihi?
When?	Impinji nyi?
Why?	Mulongadi?
Which?	Chimuchidihi?
How?	Munjila nyi?

To show respect, preface the name of the person you are talking to with 'Ba', e.g. May – Ba Mary; Mr Phiri – Ba Phiri.

GENERAL CONVERSATION

Do you speak English?	Eyi wahoshanga idime da Chingeleshi?
I don't speak Lunda	Hinahosaña Lunda ku
I speak a little Lunda	Nahoshaña Lunda lwanti
I am learning Lunda	Nidi nakudiza Lunda
Sorry, I don't understand	Sole, natiyaña wanyi
Please repeat that	Funtilakuhu cheñi
Please speak slowly	Hoshaku chovu
What is this?	Chumanyi ichi?
How do you say… in Lunda?	Mwahoshaña ngahi.. mulunda?
How do you say… in English?	Mwahoshaña ngahi… mu Chingeleshi?
Did I pronounce it right?	Nayiteni chachiwahi tahindi?
Do you understand me?	Wunakutiya iji nakuhosha?
This is my…	Iwu diyi…
Wife	Ñonda muntu

Husband	Iyala wasumbula
Son	Mwana weyala
Daughter	Mwana wamumbanda
Sister	Muhelami
Brother	Manakwami
Friend	Ibwambu
I work as a…	Nazatana…
I am… years old	Nidi nayaka yakushika ku…
Are you married?	Wasumbuka tahindi?
I am married	Nasumbuka
I am not married	Nasumbuka wanyi
How many children do you have?	Wudi nawanyana añahi?
I don't have any children	Hinidi nanyana wanyi
I have… children	Nidi nawanyana akushika ku…
I am on holiday	Nidi hampinji yakunoka
I am working here	Nidi nakuzata kunu
I live here	Nashakama hanu
Where do you come from?	Wafuma kudi?
I am from…	Nafuma ku…
Can I take a photo?	Niyikope mwevulu?
Where is the toilet?	Indi chimbushu chidi kudihi?
Entrance	Hawingililu
Exit	Njila yakufuma heluna
Ladies	Akulumpi awambanda akaleme sha
Gentlemen	Akulumpi amayala akaleme sha
Me	Yami
You	Yeyi
She	Yena
He	Yena

We	Yetu
They	Wena
I feel cold/hot	Nidi nakutiya mashika/iyena
I feel tired	Nidi nakutiya kuzeya
I am hungry and thirsty	Nidi nakutiya nzala ni mpwila
I like it here	Nidi y nakuyikeñela hanu
Mr	Mukulumpi weyala
Mrs	Mubanda wasumbuka
Miss	Izu dakuzatisha kudi mubanda wamujiki
See you later	Tukudimona mpinji yekwawu
See you tomorrow	Tukudimona kumadiki
Why?	Muloñadi?
Because…	Muloña wa…
I don't understand	Hinatiyishaña wanyi
I don't know	Neluki wanyi
I think…	Natoñojoki…
I want…	Nakeñi…
I don't want…	Hinakeni wanyi…
I like…	Nidi nakukeña…
I don't like…	Nidi nakukeña wanyi…

GETTING AROUND

Excuse me, where is…?	Ananakenuku mwani, kudihi kwekala…?
Where are the…	Kudihi kudi ma…
Shops	Yitanda
Restaurants	Matala akulandishila nakudila yakudya

Night clubs	Matala akudiwenena na mpinji ya wufuku
Where is the…?	Kudihi kudi…?
Lake	Ijiya
River	Kaloña
Village	Mukala
Game park	Dizevu da wanyama
Post Office	Itala da kutemeshela nakutambwila nyikanda
Bank	Chimbañu cha mali
Bureau de Change	Kwakuhimpila mali
Museum	Itala daku hembela yuma nakuyimwekesa kudi añenji
Church	Chimpompelu
Bus stop	Hawimenu wa bus
Train station	Hawimenu wa sitima
Airport	Ibulu da ndeki
Where is this?	Kudihi kudi ichi?
Can I walk there?	Natweshi kwenda hamaseki?
Do you have a map?	Mudiku na mwevulu?
Can you show me?	Wunatweshi kulejaku?
To the…	Ku…
Left	Chimunswa
Right	Chidilu
Straight ahead	Kwoloka hambidi
Where are you going?	Wanakuya kudihi?
I am going to…	Nidi makuya ku…
Is this the way to…?	Iyi diyi njila yakuya ku..?
I want to travel by…	Nakengi kwendela mu…
Bicycle	Nkiña

Motorbike	Katukutuku
Boat	Watu
Horse	Ngameli
Vehicle (general)	Motoka
How much does the journey cost?	Wukufwika chiñahi weniwu wuñeji?
How long will it take?	Yikusenda mpinji jiñahi?
Can I buy a ticket?	Nilandi itikiti tahi?
Where's the bus/train/plane/ boat for…?	Indi bus/sitima/ndeke/ watu yidi kudihi…?
How can I go there?	Nikutwesha kuya ku ng'ahi?
I want to see the…	Nakukena kumona…
Is there a driver?	Kudiku nyamutekenya?
Can I go today?	Niyi lelu tahindi?
Is there an entrance fee?	Kudi mali akufwetela ha chinsu?
What are the opening hours?	Indi jimpinji jakwenzununa jimp injinyi?
It's open from… to…	Enzununaña kufuma ku… nakushika ku…
Street/road	Njila/mukwakwa
A little bit	Chantesha hohu
A lot	Yayivulu
Quickly	Nyakeshenuku
Slowly	Chovu
What's the best way to…?	Injilanyi yayiwahi nakuya ku...?
Should I take a taxi?	Niyi na taxi tahindi?
It's near the …	Kwakamwihi na…
Cross the road	Kilukaku injila
Go past the…	Uhitiliku…
It's near here	Hakamwihi na hanu

It's far from here	Hahalehi kufuma hanu
It's too far to walk	Hahalehi nankashi nakwenda
It's ten minutes by foot	Yekala minyutu ikumi kwenda na nyendu
It's five minutes by car	Neyi namotoka yekalaminyutu yitanu
Do I need my passport?	Chinakukengeka chitupa tahindi?

PUBLIC TRANSPORT

Is this the right bus for…?	Iyi diyi bus yaku yaku….?
Where's the nearest bus stop?	Indi chitulilu cha bus chamwa-kamwihi chidi kudihi?
How much is the fare?	Wuseya chiñahi?
I'm going to…	Nidi nakuya ku…
Where can I drop off?	Nikasulukila kudihi?
Which bus/train can I take to..?	Bus/sitima yimu yidi nukuya nayu…?
Can I have my change?	Nyikenu change yami
Please stop here	Imanenu hanu mwani

CARS

I want to hire a car	Nakukeña kukumuna motoka
Where's the best place to rent a car?	Kudihi kwa ku wahi kwa kusonkela motoka?
I want a small/large vehicle	Nakukenga motoka yanyanya/ mweseka/yeneni
I want it today/tomorrow	Nakuchikeña lelu/kumadiki

How much do you charge?	Mwafweteshaña chingahi?
Fill it up please	Chizeshenu
The tyre's flat	Kafumbu twabasalala
It's broken down	Chinafwi
Can you fix it?	Ukuchipachika tahindi?
Is there a garage/mechanic near here?	Kudi ku garage/mukwaku lungisha kwakamwihi kunu?
When will it be ready?	Yakawaha impinji nyi?
Can you do it now?	Muzachiluhu katataka?

GAME VIEWING

We want to go somewhere on Friday	Tudi nakukeña tuyi kumu ha chitanu
There'll be two of us	Tukwikala mwayedi wetu
Is it worth seeing?	Chidi chakuzañalesha tahi?
Is it suitable for children?	Chinateli antwansi tahindi?
How much does it cost?	Yikufwika chiñahi?
What does the price include?	Yumanji cheñi yinabombewi mundandu?
What time will we leave?	Tukunyamuka mpinji nyi?
What time will we get back?	Tukufunta impinji nyi?
Is lunch included?	Anabombeluku kudya cha mwaana tahindi?
Where do I buy a ticket?	Kudihi nukulandila pasu?
Buffalo	Mpakasa
Crocodile	Chibokolu
Elephant	Nzovu
Giraffe	Tutwa
Hippopotamus	Nuvu

Lion	Mutupa
Monkey	Nsoku
Rhinoceros	Insontu
Snake	Inoka
Zebra	Ngolo

AT THE HOTEL

I want a good hotel	Nidi nakukeña itala dakushinkena dadiwahi
Do you have a room available?	Mudiku netala dakuloñesha dehi?
I want a room for… people	Nidi nakukeñaku itala da wantu a…
With a nice view	Nakumwekana chiwahi
For one night/two nights/ one week	Naufuku wumu/ufuku wuyedi/ mulungu wumu
I've made a reservation	Niku hembelaku
My name is…	Ijina dami yami…
How much is a room?	Kabeta kamu kadi chiñahi?
Is breakfast included?	Kudya chantetemena nichena muna chishiluku tahindi?
Is it air conditioned?	Inshakaminu ya mpepela tahi?
You are in room number…	Eyi wudi mukabeta ya nambala..
Please give me a wake-up call at	Wakahindwishi ku shinga mapinji ya…
Is there a restaurant here?	Kudiku itala dakunwina nakudya?
Is there a…	Kudiku chi…
Swimming pool	Dawa dakuwelela
Gym	Kukiluka nakudibalumuna

Hairdressers	Antu akwakutewula nsuki neyi mudimu wawu
Gift shop	Chitanda chamawana
Night club	Izanvu dawantu akudiwana nakuhema nakunwa nampinji ya wufuku
Business centre	Hakachi kelunga dakusekashana?
Room service	Kabeta kakuzatila mwitala
Please bring… to my room	Nentenu kunu kukabeta… kami
Please bring my luggage	Nentenu chisenda chami
Are there any messages for me?	Kudiku mazu anami?
I want bed and breakfast only	Nakukeña kadidi na kudya chantetemena hohu
I want lunch included	Nakukeña kudya chamwaana kushilaku ni
Porter	Muntu wasendana yola na yuma yawakwawu yacheni
Please help with my bags	Nkwashenuku kusenda yola yami
It's heavy	Chinalemi
Please fetch me a taxi	Mwani akengeluku taxi

SHOPPING

At the…	Ha…
Market	Chisankanu
Shop	Chitanda
Grocers	Yuma neyi losu, makundi, menzhi atata na coffee
Chemist	Itala dakulandishila yitumbu
Gift shop	Chitanda chamawana

I want one	Nakukeña chimu
Give me this/these, please	Nyinkaku ichi/iji
How much is it?	Chidi useya chinahi?
That's too expensive	Useya unasweji
Can you lower the price?	Wukufumishaku wuseya?
Have you got anything cheaper?	Wudiku nayuma yimu yawuseya wantesha?
It's nice/beautiful	Chachiwahi/chinawahi nankashi
I like it	Nachikeñi
I don't like it	Nachikeñi wanyi
Yes, please	Eña mwani
No, thank you	Nehi, nasakilili
Do you sell…?	Walandishaña…?
Here's the money	Tambula mali anu
Have you got change for this?	Wudi na change ya niyi?
Please can I have my change?	Nyinkenu change yami?
I'll buy it	Nikuchilanda
How many?	Yiñahi?
I don't have enough money	Hinikweti mali ashikilamuku
It's too big/small	Chinatohi/chinakehi nankashi
Do you have it in my size?	Wudi nayakweseka mumali ami?
Do you have it in this colour?	Wudiku nayamuchidi neyi iyi?
I want a/some…	Nakukeñaku…
Can I try this/these on?	Nesekiku ichi/iyi?
I need a receipt	Nidi nakukeña pasu

Sometimes you can swap things for goods, e.g. a t-shirt could be used as part payment towards a souvenir.

AT THE POST OFFICE

Where is the Post Office?	Indi itala dakutemeshela nyikanda didi kudihi?
How much is a stamp for…?	Stampa yimu… chiñahi?
I want to send this letter/ parcel to…	Nakukena kutemesha iwu mukanda kudi/mpasha…
Five stamps for letters/ postcards to… please	Masitampa atanu ya nyikanda/ makadi akutemeshela mwani...
Where can I post them?	Nikuyitemeshela kudihi?
Please give me an airmail envelope	Munyinkenku envelope ya kutemeshela mukanda
Do you sell airmail writing paper?	Mwalandishanga mapepal akusonekela?

IN A RESTAURANT/CAFÉ

I want a table for… people	Nidi nakukeña mesa ya… antu
Near the window	Kwakamwihi na njanena
I want to eat…	Nakukeña kudya…
I want to drink…	Nakukeña kunwa…
Breakfast	Kudya cha ntetemena
Lunch	Kudya cha mwaana
Dinner	Kudya cha melela
Snack	Snack
What's the speciality?	Chumanyi mwelukisha nankashi?
What do you recommend?	Wukwiteja chumanyi?
Knife	Mpoku
Fork	Fwoloku
Spoon	Ngutu

Plate	Cheña
Cup	Mpasa
Glass	Chinbanjilu
Dish	Mbashila
I've made a reservation	Nichidi nakutalilaku
My name is…	Ijina dami yami…
That's not what I ordered	Hidimu naloneshaku
Dinner is ready	Kudya cheneni chinawaheshiwi dehi
Can I have some more of this, please?	Nyinkenuku cheng'i yikwawu?
Can I see the menu/wine list?	Nitaluku ipepa dawuseya wa yakudya/walwa?
I'd like to have a…	Nakukeng'a kwikala na…
What drinks do you have?	Yakunwanyi wudi nayu?
Where can I get a drink?	Kudi nikuwana yakunwa?
Would you like tea or coffee?	Wukukeng'a chayi tahindi kofi?
I'll have a beer please	Nyinkenu walwa mwani
One cup of coffee	Lumpasa lumu lwa kofi
Cheers!	Kuhameka!
Can I have some salt, please	Nyinkenuku mung'wa mwani
This is delicious	Iyi yayiwahi
I don't want anything else	Hinakukeng'a yacheng'i wanyi
The bill, please	Awayishi ja kufweta

FOOD AND DRINK

Food	Yakudya
Coffee	Kofi
Tea	Chayi

Beer	Walwa
Water	Menji
Beef	Mbiji ya ngulu
Pork	Mbiji ya ng'ombi
Chicken	Kasumbi
Fish	Inshi
Maize	Kabaaka
Tomato	Machamacha
Okra	Mwilembu wanyi vunu
Pumpkin leaves	Mafu achi bwabwa
Beans	Makundi
Rice	Losu
Sweet potato	Ntaamba
Onion	Sapola
Salt	Mungwa
Sugar	Sukili
Cold	Chishika
Hot	Iyena
Sweet	Kutowala
Spicy	Iwundu hela muji ashang'awu kuyakudya kulonda yitowali

The staple food in Zambia is nshima, *made with mealie meal, served with relish and eaten with your hands.*

GETTING HELP

Help!	Kukwasha!
Call the police	Tambikenu atu pokola!
I need an ambulance	Nakeni ambulance

I feel ill	Nidi nakuti ya kukata
I've been robbed	Analukuki
I need a doctor	Nakeni ndotolu
My… hurts	Nedikatishi…
Head	Mutu
Stomach	Ivumu
Arm	Chikasa
Leg	Mwendu
Back	Nyima
It hurts here	Chidi nakkukatila hanu
I can't sleep	Nikutwesha kukama wanyi
I'm feeling worse	Nakutiya wunu chinasweji
I'm feeling better	Nakutiyaku wunu chiwahi
Take me to the…	Ntwalenu ku…
Hospital	Chipatela
Doctor	Ndotolu
Police	Chiwanyino chatupokola
I've lost my passport	Najimbeshi pasu
My money's been stolen	Mali ami anayiyi
I left it in my room/on the bus	Nayishi ya mwitala dami/ha bus
Is there someone who can help me?	Kudihu muntu natweshi kungukwasha?
It's an emergency	Chakukasumwisha
We need help urgently	Tunakukeng'a wukwashi swayi swayi
Call the police/ambulance/ fire brigade	Tambikenu atupokola/ ambulance/ nawakwakujima kesi
Where are you?	Wudi kudihi?
I'm at…	Nidi ha…
What's happened?	Kunawudiki chumanyi?

There's been an accident/a fire	Kunadini mpondi/kakesi
It's serious	Inasweji nankashi

To call for help, dial 999 and state which sort of assistance you require.

DAYS, TIME AND WEATHER

Monday	Chimu
Tuesday	Chiyedi
Wednesday	Chisatu
Thursday	Chiwana
Friday	Chitanu
Saturday	Satela
Sunday	Mulungu
Today	Lelu
Yesterday	Haloshi
Tomorrow	Kumadiki
Last week	Mulungu wunamani
Last month	Kakweji iwu namani
Last year	Hamwakadi
Next week	Mulungu wukwinzahu
Next month	Kakweji wukwinzahu
Next year	Kumwakadi
Morning	Ntetemena
Afternoon	Na mwaana
Evening	Melela
Night	Ufuku
See you tomorrow!	Twakadimona kumadiki!
See you on Friday!	Twakadimon da chitanu!

Now	Yoyena inu mpinji
Then	Dichi
Later	Mpinji yekwawu
Before	Henohu kanda
After	Ha kukumisha
What time is it?	Yidi mpinji nyi?
It's… o'clock	Yidi mpinji ya…

Zambia uses the twenty-four clock in telling the time, e.g. 6pm – 18:00 hours.

What's the weather like?	Kudi nakutiyangana ngahi?
It's hot	Kudi iyena chanti
It's cold	Kudi chishika
It's rainy	Kudi mvula
It's windy	Kudi mpepela

NUMBERS AND MONEY

One	Chimu
Two	Yiyedi
Three	Yisatu
Four	Yiwana
Five	Yitanu
Six	Yitanu na chimu
Seven	Yitanu na yiyedi
Eight	Yitanu na yisatu
Nine	Yitanu na yiwana
Ten	Ikumi

For higher numbers, use English.
The Zambian currency is Kwacha and Ngwee.

VERBS

To be	
I am	Nidi
You (familiar/single) are	Udi na
S/he is	Wudi na
We are	Tudi na
You (polite/plural) are	Mudi na
They are	Adi na
To have	**Kwikala machu**
I have	Nidi na
You (familiar/single) have	Udi na
S/he has	Wudi na
We have	Tudi na
You (polite/plural) have	Mudi na
They have	Adi na
To want	**Kukenga**
I want	Nakukena
You (familiar/single) want	Unakukenga
S/he wants	Wudi nakukena
We want	Tunakeni
You (polite/plural) want	Munakukenga
They want	Anakukena

To like

I like	Nakeng'a
You (familiar/single) like	Wakenga
S/he likes	Wakena
We like	Twakena
You (polite/plural) like	Mwakenga
They like	Akena

VERB LIST

To go	Kuya
To come	Kwinza
To eat	Kudya
To drink	Kunwa
To sleep	Kukamama
To walk	Kwenda
To buy	Kulanda
To see	Kumona
To stay	Kushakama
To stop	Kukumisha
To travel	Kwenda
To pay	Kufweta
To choose	Kusakula
To help	Kukwasha
To cook	Kuteleka
To rest	Kumoka
To feel	Natiyi
To speak	Kuhosha
To give	Kuhana
To ask	Kwihula

To know	Kwihuka
To think	Kutongojoka
To be happy	Kutiya muzangalo

LUVALE

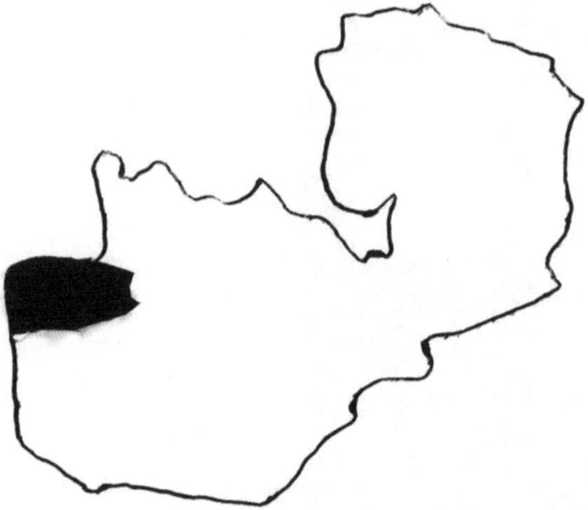

The Luvale-speaking people of Zambia live mainly in the North-Western Province.

'Hanjikila wevwa hikila wekuta'
Talk to a person who can understand and cook for a person who can be satisfied

GREETINGS AND FIRST WORDS

Hello	Ngachilihi
How are you?	Munayoyo mwane
I'm fine. And you?	Nguli kanawa, ngachili yove nawa?
Fine, thank you	Kanawa mwane
Good morning	Hinukkeni mwane
Good afternoon	Chingolashi mwane
Good night	Musa vale mwane
Goodbye	Salenuho mwane
See you!	Naulimona!
Yes	Eyo
No	Pimbi
Maybe	Pamo
Okay/fine	Eyo chamwaza
Excuse me	Lusesa mwane
Sorry	Ngukonekelenuko
Thank you very much	Tunasakwilila chikuma
What's your name?	Lijina lyove yove hiya?
My name is…	Lijina lyami yami…
Pleased to meet you	Tunawahilila kuliwana nayove
Please come in	Ingilenu mwane
Please sit down	Twamenu mwane
Welcome	Tambokenu mwane

Please can you help me?	Ngukafwenuko mwane?
Who?	Hiya?
What?	Yika?
Where?	Kulihi?
When?	Lwola muka?
Why?	Momo ika?
Which?	Mujila muka?
How?	Ngachilihi?

To show respect, preface the name of the person you are talking to with 'Ba', e.g. May – Ba Mary; Mr Phiri – Ba Phiri.

GENERAL CONVERSATION

Do you speak English?	Wechi kuhanjikanga chingeleshi tahi?
I don't speak Luvale	Kangwechi kuhanjika Luvaleko
I speak a little Luvale	Ngwechi kuhanjikanga Luvale chindende kaha
I am learning Luvale	Nguli nakulilongesa Luvale
Sorry, I don't understand	Ngukonekelenuko, kangwevwileko
Please repeat that	Hilukilenuho cheka mwane
Please speak slowly	Hanjikenu mwane chindende
What is this?	Chuma mukechi?
How do you say… in Luvale?	Mwechi kuvulukanga ngachilihi… muluvale?
How do you say… in English?	Mwechi kwanbanga ngachilihi… mu chingeleshi?

Did I pronounce it right?	Ngunachihanjika mwakwoloka tahi?
Do you understand me?	Unakwivwa omu ngunakuhanjika?
This is my…	Ou ikiye…
Wife	Pwevo lyami
Husband	Lunga lyami
Son	Mwanami walunga
Daughter	Mwanami wapwevo
Sister	Ndumbu
Brother	Mwana kwavo
Friend	Sepa lyami
Family	Tanga yami
I work as a…	Ngwazata mulimo wa…
I am… years old	Nguli namyaka ya…
Are you married?	Wasomboka tahi?
I am married	Ngwasomboka
I am not married	Kangwasombokako
How many children do you have?	Uli navana vangahi?
I don't have any children	Kangweshi navanako
I have… children	Nguli navana va…
I am on holiday	Nguli ha kunoka
I am working here	Nguli nakuzata hano
I live here	Ngwatwama kuno
Where do you come from?	Wafuma kulihi?
I am from…	Ngwafuma ku…
Can I take a photo?	Ngunahase kukopa muvwimbimbi?
Where is the toilet?	Chimbushu chili kuli hi?
Entrance	Wingililo

Exit	Ulovokelo
Ladies	Vaka mama
Gentlemen	Vaka tata
Me	Yami
You	Yove
She	Ove pwevo
He	Ove lunga
We	Yetu
They	Vakiko
I feel cold/hot	Nguli nakwivwa chishika/liyena
I feel tired	Nguli nakwivwa kuzeya
I am hungry and thirsty	Nguli nakwivwa zala na lipwila
I like it here	Ngunazangeko kuno
Mr	Mwata
Mrs	Mukazuvo ya
Miss	Mujike
See you later	Natulimona lwola lweka
See you tomorrow	Natukali mona hamene
Why?	Mwomwo ika?
Because…	Mwomwo…
I don't understand	Kangwechi kwivwishisako
I don't know	Kangwatachikijileko
I think…	Ngunashinganyeka…
I want…	Ngunazange…
I don't want…	Kangwazangileko…
I like…	Ngwazanga…
I don't like…	Kangwazanga…

GETTING AROUND

Excuse me, where is…?	Nguhuliseko mwane, kuhihi..?
Where are the…?	Kulihi kuli vi…?
Shops	Vitanda
Restaurants	Jizuvo jakulanjila vyakulya
Night clubs	Mazavo akuliwanyina vatu ufuku?
Where is the…?	Kulihi kuli…?
Lake	Chijiva
River	Kalwiji
Village	Limbo
Game park	Livundu
Post Office	Poshita
Bank	Vanki
Bureau de Change	Kwakuchenjela mali aku mafuchi eka
Museum	Zuvo yakulamina vyuma naku vimwenesa kuli vangeji
Church	Liuka
Bus stop	Chitulilo chaji bus
Train station	Chitulilo cha sitima
Airport	Chivaza cha ndeki
Where is this?	Kulihi kuli echi?
Can I walk there?	Ngunahase kutambuka?
Do you have a map?	Uliko na map?
Can you show me?	Unahase kungumwenesa?
To the…	Ku…
Left	Chimoswe
Right	Chilyo
Straight ahead	Kusungama hakulutwe

Where are you going?	Uli nakuya kulihi?
I am going to…	Nguli nakuya ku…
Is this the way to…?	Eyi yikiko jila yakuya ku…?
I want to travel by…	Ngunakutonda kuya na…
Bicycle	Kinga
Motorbike	Mutukutuku
Boat	Wato
Horse	Kavalu
Vehicle (general)	Mingawu
How much does the journey cost?	Nayifwika chingahi eyi jila?
How long will it take?	Nayimbata lwola lungahi?
Can I buy a ticket?	Ngulande litikiti tahi?
Where's the bus/train/ boat/plane for…?	Yilikulihi bus/sitima/wato yaku-wato bwaku/nedeke..?
How can I go there?	Nanguyako ngachilihi kuze?
I want to see the…	Ngwakutonda kumona…
Is there a driver?	Kuli nyamutekenya?
Can I go today?	Nguyenga lelo tahi?
Is there an entrance fee?	Kuli mali akufwetela hachikolo?
What are the opening hours?	Jilwola jakusokolola, jilwola muka?
It's open from… to…	Veji kusokola kufuma ha… nakuneha kulwola lwa…
Street/road	Mukwakwa/tapalo
A little bit	Chindende kaha
A lot	Vyavivulu
Quickly	Washi-washi
Slowly	Chikoki
What's the best way to…?	Jila muka yamwaza ya ku…?
Should I take a taxi?	Nguyenga na taxi tahi?

It's near the …	Yili hakamwihi na…
Cross the road	Zomboka mukwakwa
Go past the…	Hichila ha…
It's near here	Yili hakamwini hano
It's far from here	Yili kwakusuku na kuno
It's too far to walk	Kuli kwakusuku chikuma kutam buka hamavu
It's ten minutes by foot	Yili minyutu likumi kutambu ka hamahinji
It's five minutes by car	Yili minyutu yitanu na minyau
Do I need my passport?	Chinakuzangiwa chitupa chami tahi?

PUBLIC TRANSPORT

Is this the right bus for…?	Eyi yikiko bus yakuya ku…?
Where's the nearest bus stop?	Chitulilo cha bus chamwakamwihi chili kuli?
How much is the fare?	Ndando yili chingahi?
I'm going to…	Nguli nakuya ku…
Where can I drop off?	Nanga sulukila halihi?
Which bus/train can I take to..?	Sitima/bus muka nangunyina nakuya ku…?
Can I have my change?	Nguhanenu change yami?
Please stop here	Imanenu hano mwane

CARS

I want to hire a car	Ngunakuzanga kukumuna mingawu
Where's the best place to rent a car?	Kulihi kuli ngalila yamwaza nakutela mingawu?
I want a small/large vehicle	Ngunazange minyawu yiyindende/yayinene
I want it today/tomorrow	Ngunakuyizanga lelo lino/ hamene
How much do you charge?	Munakufwetesa chingahi?
Fill it up please	Yizalisenu mwane
The tyre's flat	Lifumbo lina popoloka
It's broken down	Yinafu
Can you fix it?	Nauhasa kuyilungisa?
Is there a garage/mechanic near here?	Natuwanako garage/machanyika kwaka mwihi kuno?
When will it be ready?	Nayipwa kanawa lwola muka?
Can you do it now?	Nauhasa kuchilinga oholili vene ngana?

GAME VIEWING

We want to go somewhere on Friday	Natuzanga kuyako kumwe ha chitanu
There'll be two of us	Natukapwa tuvavali
Is it worth seeing?	Kuli kwambwende kuya naku monako?
Is it suitable for children?	Kuli kwakanawa hamwe navanyike?

How much does it cost?	Nayifwika chingahi?
What does the price include?	Vyuma muka vilimo mundando eyi?
What time will we leave?	Natukatuka lwwola muka?
What time will we get back?	Natuhiluka lwola muka?
Is lunch included?	Kulya chamusana muchili tahi?
Where do I buy a ticket?	Kulihi nangulanda pasu?
Buffalo	Pakasa
Crocodile	Ngandu
Elephant	Njamba
Giraffe	Tungu
Hippopotamus	Nguvu
Lion	Ndumba
Monkey	Soko
Rhinoceros	Soto
Snake	Linoka
Zebra	Ngolo

AT THE HOTEL

I want a good hotel	Ngunakutonda zuvo yakushikishila yamwaza
Do you have a room available?	Uliko na zuvo yakutamo?
I want a room for… people	Nguli nakutonda zuvo ya vatu va..
With a nice view	Nakusoloka kanawa
For one night/two nights/ one week	Ufuku umwe/maufuku avali/ chalumingo chimwe
I've made a reservation	Ngunalizange nakutumbika
My name is…	Lijina lyami yami…
How much is a room?	Kapeka kamwe chingahi?

Is breakfast included?	Kulya chachimene nachikiko kuchili?
Is it air conditioned?	Muli likina lya peho?
You are in room number…	Uli mu chihanda cha nambala...
Please give me a wake-up call at	Ukanguhindwise ha…
Is there a restaurant here?	Kuliko zuvo yakulila hano?
Is there a…	Kuliko…
Swimming pool	Lyawu
Gym	Kulyalumuna
Hairdressers	Mwaku wahishila jikambu
Gift shop	Chitanda chamawana
Night club	Zuvo yakuliwanyina na ufuku
Business centre	Hakachi kakusekasanyika
Room service	Kuneha kuzuvo yami
Please bring… to my room	Nehenu ku zuvo yami…
Please bring my luggage	Nehenu mwane chiteli chami
Are there any messages for me?	Kuliko mijimbu yami?
I want bed and breakfast only	Ngunazange kahela nakulya chachimene kaha
I want lunch included	Ngunazanga kuhakilako kulya chamusana
Porter	Mutu mukakumbata viteli
Please help with my bags	Ngukafweko viteli vyami
It's heavy	Chachilemu
Please fetch me a taxi	Ngutondeleko minyawu yakungu mbatako

SHOPPING

At the…	Ha…
Market	Chisakano
Shop	Chitanda
Grocers	Vakakulanjisa
Chemist	Muchitanda chakulanjishila vitumbo
Gift shop	Chitanda chamawana
I want one	Nunakuzangako chimwe
Give me this/these, please	Nguhane echi/evi mwane
How much is it?	Ndando ili chingahi?
That's too expensive	Ndando inatoho chikuma
Can you lower the price?	Tepululako ndando?
Have you got anything cheaper?	Uliko navimwe vyandando yayindende?
It's nice/beautiful	Chamwaza chikuma
I like it	Ngunachizange
I don't like it	Kagwachizangileko
Yes, please	Eyo, mwane
No, thank you	Pimbi, mwane
Do you sell…?	Wechi kulanjisa tahi…?
Here's the money	Mali ano
Have you got change for this?	Uli na change ya awa?
Please can I have my change?	Nguhane change yami?
I'll buy it	Nanguchilanda
How many?	Vingahi?
I don't have enough money	Kangweshi namali akutamoko
It's too big/small	Yinatoho chikuma/yinakehe chikuma

Do you have it in my size?	Muli nayo nguahase kutamo?
Do you have it in this colour?	Uliko na yeyi yamuwulo omu?
I want a/some…	Ngunaku tondako/vimwe…
Can I try this/these on?	Ngwesekeko echi/evi?
I need a receipt	Ngunakutonda unguhane kalipepa

Sometimes you can swap things for goods, e.g. a t-shirt could be used as part payment towards a souvenir.

AT THE POST OFFICE

Where is the Post Office?	Post Office ili kuli?
How much is a stamp for…?	Stamp imwe vanakulinga… chingahi?
I want to send this letter/ parcel to…	Ngunakutonda kutumisa ou mukanda/pasha kuli…
Five stamps for letters/ postcards to… please	Ma sitampa atanu amikanda/ mapepa akutumisa… mwane
Where can I post them?	Nanguyipositala kulihi?
Please give me an airmail envelope	Nguhanenuko chakutumishila mikanda na ndeki
Do you sell airmail writing paper?	Mweji kulanjisanga mapepa aku sonekela?

IN A RESTAURANT/CAFÉ

I want a table for… people	Nguli nakutonda mesa yakuheta muvatu va…
Near the window	Kwakamwihi na njamena
I want to eat…	Ngunakusaka kulya…
I want to drink…	Ngunakusaka kunwa…
Breakfast	Chakulya chachimene
Lunch	Chakulya chamusana
Dinner	Chakulya cha chingoloshi
Snack	Twakulya mwane
What's the speciality?	Kulya chauhashi chalelo chika?
What do you recommend?	Chamwaza chili naungusakwila?
Knife	Poko
Fork	Fwoloko
Spoon	Nguto
Plate	Lilonga
Cup	Lupasa
Glass	Ngilasi
Dish	Chenga
I've made a reservation	Ngunalizange nakutumbika
My name is…	Lijina lyami yami…
That's not what I ordered	Echi keshi chikiko ngwashikisangako
Dinner is ready	Kulya cha ufuku chinahi lyehi
Can I have some more of this, please?	Nguhanenuko vikwavo vyovimwe cheka, mwane?
Can I see the menu/wine list?	Ngutaleko lipepa lyakusoneka vyakulya/wala?
I'd like to have a…	Ngunakuzangako…

What drinks do you have?	Muli navyakunwa muka?
Where can I get a drink?	Kulihi nanguwanako vyakunwa?
Would you like tea or coffee?	Nauznagako tiyi tahi nyi coffee?
I'll have a beer please	Nanguzanga wala mwane
One cup of coffee	Lupasa lumwe lwa coffee
Cheers!	Tuwahililenu mwane!
Can I have some salt, please	Nguhanenuko mungwa mwane
This is delicious	Evi viyema
I don't want anything else	Kangwazangile vyekako
The bill, please	Lipepa lyandando mwane

FOOD AND DRINK

Food	Vyakulya
Coffee	Coffee
Tea	Tiyi
Beer	Wala
Water	Meya
Beef	Nyama
Pork	Nyama ya ngulu
Chicken	Kasumbi
Fish	Vaishi
Maize	Chivwale
Tomato	Macha macha
Okra	Chingombwa
Pumpkin leaves	Mafwo a mapungu
Beans	Makunde
Rice	Loso
Sweet potato	Tamba
Onion	Sapwola

Salt	Mungwa
Sugar	Sukili
Cold	Kututa
Hot	Yakakahya
Sweet	Kuyema

The staple food in Zambia is nshima*, made with mealie meal, served with relish and eaten with your hands.*

GETTING HELP

Help!	Kafwenu!
Call the police	Tambikenu kapokola!
I need an ambulance	Ngunazange ambulance
I feel ill	Nguli nakwivwa kukola
I've been robbed	Vanangwivila
I need a doctor	Ngunakutonda ndotolo
My… hurts	Ha… hanakukola
Head	Mutwe
Stomach	Lijimo
Arm	Livoko
Leg	Lihinji
Back	Nyima
It hurts here	Chinakukolela aha
I can't sleep	Tulo twauchi
I'm feeling worse	Nguli nakwivwa uno chinasweze
I'm feeling better	Nguili nakwivwako uno kanawa
Take me to the…	Ngutwalenu ku…
Hospital	Chipatela
Doctor	Ndotolo

Police	Tupokola
I've lost my passport	Ngunajimbalisa chitupa chami
My money's been stolen	Mali ami vanawevi
I left it in my room/on the bus	Ngwayisezanga muzuvo yami/ mu bus
Is there someone who can help me?	Kuli umwe mwjahasa kungukafwako?
It's an emergency	Chili chakuzanguwisa washi
We need help urgently	Tunakutonda kutukafwa washi washi
Call the police/ambulance/ fire brigade	Tambikenu tupokola/ambulance/ vakakujima kakahya
Where are you?	Uli kulihi?
I'm at…	Nguli ha…
What's happened?	Chuma muka chinalingika?
There's been an accident/a fire	Kunasoloka ponde/kakahya
It's serious	Chinasweze chikuma

To call for help, dial 999 and state which sort of assistance you require.

DAYS, TIME AND WEATHER

Monday	Chimwe
Tuesday	Chivali
Wednesday	Chitatu
Thursday	Chiwana
Friday	Chitanu
Saturday	Sateli
Sunday	Chalumingo

Today	Lelo
Yesterday	Zawu
Tomorrow	Hamene
Last week	Chalumingo chapwangaho
Last month	Kakweji apwangaho
Last year	Mwaka wali
Next week	Chalumingo nachizaho
Next month	Kakweji mwezaho
Next year	Kushikako
Morning	Chimene
Afternoon	Chingoloshi
Evening	Chiteuko
Night	Ufuku
See you tomorrow!	Natukalimona hamene!
See you on Friday!	Natukalimona lya chitanu!
Now	Oholili
Then	Jino
Later	Lwola lukwavo
Before	Shimbu kanda
After	Hanyima
What time is it?	Lwola muka?
It's… o'clock	Lwola luli…

Zambia uses the twenty-four clock in telling the time, e.g. 6pm – 18:00 hours.

What's the weather like?	Ngonde yili ngachilihi?
It's hot	Kuli liyena
It's cold	Kuli chishika
It's rainy	Kuli vula
It's windy	Kuli peho

NUMBERS AND MONEY

One	Chimwe
Two	Vivali
Three	Vitatu
Four	Viwana
Five	Vitanu
Six	Vitanu na chimwe
Seven	Vitanu na vivali
Eight	Vitanu na vitatu
Nine	Vitanu na viwana
Ten	Likumi

For higher numbers, use English.
The Zambian currency is Kwacha and Ngwee.

VERBS

To be	**Na chi kapwa ngana**
I am	Yami
You (familiar/single) are	Yove
S/he is	Yikiye
We are	Yetu
You (polite/plural) are	Yenu va
They are	Vali va

To have	**Nguli**
I have	Nguli na
You (familiar/single) have	Uli na
S/he has	Ali na
We have	Tuli na
You (polite/plural) have	Muli na
They have	Na

To want	**Kuzanga**
I want	Ngunazange
You (familiar/single) want	Uli na kuzanga
S/he wants	Nazange
We want	Tulinakuzanga
You (polite/plural) want	Mulinakuzanga
They want	Vali nakuzanga

To like	**Kuzanga**
I like	Ngwazanga
You (familiar/single) like	Wazangwa
S/he likes	Azanga
We like	Twazanga
You (polite/plural) like	Mwazanga
They like	Vazanga

VERB LIST

To go	Kuya
To come	Kwiza
To eat	Kulya
To drink	Kunwa
To sleep	Kusavala
To walk	Kutambuka
To buy	Kulanda
To see	Kumona
To stay	Kutwama
To stop	Kwimana
To travel	Kuya
To pay	Kufweta
To choose	Kusakula
To help	Kukafwe
To cook	Kuteleka
To rest	Kunoka
To feel	Kwivwa
To speak	Kuhanjika
To give	Kuhana
To ask	Kuhulisa
To know	Kutachikiza
To think	Kushinganyeka
To be happy	Kuwalahilila

NYANJA

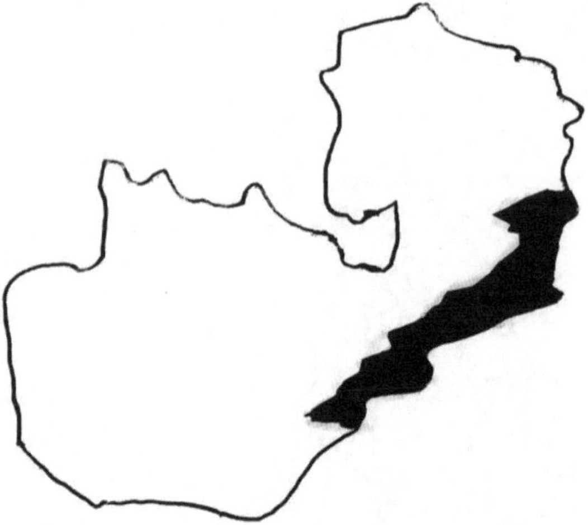

The Nyanja-speaking people of Zambia live mainly in the Eastern Province, but the language is widely spoken in Lusaka and Central Province and can be understood almost anywhere in the country.

'Ukaipa dziwa kuvina'
If you are ugly, know how to dance

Nyanja is the language spoken most widely in Lusaka, and its use in the city has evolved into a corrupt form of the language known as 'town Nyanja'. Town Nyanja borrows words from other local languages as well as English. If you are stuck, try using the phrases below and adding your own English word with a vowel on the end, e.g. to say 'I want some bread', try saying 'Ndifuna bredi'. For 'I am a doctor', try saying 'Ndine doctoro'. The town Nyanja words are 'buledi' and 'doctolo', so you can see how easily you will be understood!

GREETINGS AND FIRST WORDS

Hello	Bwanji
How are you?	Muli bwanji?
I'm fine. And you?	Ndili bwino. Kaya inu?
Fine, thank you	Ndili bwino, zikomo
Good morning	Mwauka bwanji
Good afternoon	Machoma bwanji
Good night	Gonani bwino
Goodbye	Pitani bwino/salani bwino
See you!	Tiza onana!
Yes	Inde
No	Ai/iyai
Maybe	Kapena
Okay/fine	Chabwino

Excuse me	Zikomo
Sorry	Pepani
Thank you very much	Zikomo kwambiri
What's your name?	Dzina lanu ndani?
My name is…	Dzina langa ndine…
Pleased to meet you	Cabwino kukuziwani
Please come in	Lowani
Please sit down	Khalani pansi
Welcome	Fikani
Please can you help me?	Kodi munganithandizeko?
Who?	Ndani?
What?	Chiani?
Where?	Kuti?
When?	Liti?
Why?	Chifukwa?
Which?	Chiti?
How?	Bwanji?

To show respect, preface the name of the person you are talking to with 'Ba', e.g. May – Ba Mary; Mr Phiri – Ba Phiri.

GENERAL CONVERSATION

Do you speak English?	Mukamba Chizungu?
I don't speak Nyanja	Sindilankhula Chinyanja
I speak a little Nyanja	Ndilankhula Chinyanja pang'ono
I am learning Nyanja	Ndipunzira Chinyanja
Sorry, I don't understand	Pepani, sindimvera
Please repeat that	Pepani bwerezanso

Please speak slowly	Pepani, simungalankhuleko pang'ono pang'ono
What is this?	Nichiani ichi?
How do you say… in Nyanja?	Mukuti bwanji… mu Chinyanja?
How do you say… in English?	Mukuti bwanji… mu Chizungu?
Did I pronounce it right?	Kodi ndinanena bwino?
Do you understand me?	Kodi mundimvetsa?
This is my…	Ili ndi…
Wife	Mkazi wanga
Husband	Mwamuna wanga
Son	Mwana wanga mwamuna
Daughter	Mwana wanga mkazi
Sister	Mbuuba mbumba
Brother	Nkhoswe
Friend	M'nzanga
Family	Banja
I work as a…	Ndigwira nchito ya…
I am… years old	Ndilindi zaka…
Are you married? *(to a woman)*	Kodi muli wokwatiwa?
Are you married? *(to a man)*	Kodi muli wokwatira?
I am married *(woman)*	Ndine wokwatiwa
I am married *(man)*	Ndine wokwatira
I am not married *(woman)*	Sindine wokwatiwa
I am not married *(man)*	Sindine wokwatira
How many children do you have?	Muli ndi ana angati?
I don't have any children	Ndiribe ana
I have… children	Ndiri ndi ana…
I am on holiday	Ndili pa chuti
I am working here	Ndigwila nchito pano
I live here	Ndikhala kuno

Where do you come from?	Kodi ndiwe wakuti?
I am from…	Ndine wa ku…
Can I take a photo?	Kodi ndinga kukopeni?
Where is the toilet?	Kodi chimbuzi chilikuti?
Entrance	Pongenela
Exit	Potulukila
Ladies	Azimai
Gentlemen	Azibambo
Me	Ine
You	Iwe
She	Uyu
He	Uyu
We	Ife
They	Iwo
I feel cold/hot	Ndibvela mphepo/kupya
I feel tired	Ndimvera kulema
I am hungry and thirsty	Ndibvela njala ndi ludzu
I like it here	Ndakondako kuno
Mr	Bambo
Mrs	Amai
Miss	Amai
See you later!	Tidza onana!
See you tomorrow!	Tidza onana mawa!
Why?	Chifukwa?
Because…	Chifukwa…
I don't understand	Sindimvera
I don't know	Sindiziwa
I think…	Ndiganiza…
I want…	Ndifuna…
I don't want…	Sindifuna…

I like…	Ndikonda…
I don't like…	Sindikonda…

GETTING AROUND

Excuse me, where is…?	Zikomo, ndi kuti ku…?
Where are the…?	Ndi kuti ku…?
Shops	Masitolo
Restaurants	Mogulazakudya
Night clubs	Kumalo akumwa ndi kuvina
Where is the…?	Ndi kuti ku..
Lake	Nyanja
River	Mtsinje
Village	Mudzi
Game park	Kumalo okhalako nyama
Post Office	Post Office
Bank	Bank
Bureau de Change	Malo wosinthilako ndalama
Museum	Museum
Church	Chalichi
Bus stop	Chiteshe cha basi
Train station	Chiteshe cha sitiima
Airport	Bwalo la ndeke
Where is this?	Ndikuti kuli ichi?
Can I walk there?	Kodi ndinga yende kuja?
Do you have a map?	Kodi muli ndi mapu?
Can you show me?	Kodi mungathe kundionesa?
To the…	Pitani…
Left	Kumanzele
Right	Kulamanja

Straight ahead	Pitani pasogolo
Where are you going?	Mupita kuti?
I am going to…	Ndipita ku…
Is this the way to…?	Kodi iyi ndinjila yaku…?
I want to travel by…	Ndifuna kuyenda pa…
Bicycle	Njinga
Motorbike	Njinga yamoto
Boat	Bwato
Horse	Bulu
Vehicle (general)	Galimoto
How much does the journey cost?	Dzingati ulendo?
How long will it take?	Uzatenga nthawi bwanji?
Can I buy a ticket?	Kodi ndinga-the kugula tikiti?
Where's the bus/train/plane/ boat for…?	Kodi basi/sitima/ndeke/ bwato yaku… ili kuti?
How can I go there?	Ndinga pite bwanji kuja?
I want to see the…	Ndifuna kuona…
Is there a driver?	Pali dalaiva?
Can I go today?	Kodi ndinga pite lero?
Is there an entrance fee?	Kodi ndikulipila?
What are the opening hours?	Amatsegula nthawi bwanji?
It's open from… to…	Nkosegula kuchokela.. kufikila..
Street/road	Njila
A little bit	Pang'ono
A lot	Kwambiri
Quickly	Mwam'sanga
Slowly	Pang'ono pang'ono
What's the best way to…?	Ndi iti njila yabwino kupita ku..?
Should I take a taxi?	Kodi ndipite ndi taxi?
It's near the …	Ndipafupi ndi…

Cross the road	Lumpani njila
Go past the…	Mupitile pa…
It's near here	Ndipafupi ndi pano
It's far from here	Ndipatali ndipano
It's too far to walk	Ndipatali kuyenda
It's ten minutes by foot	Ndi mpindi khumi kuyenda
It's five minutes by car	Ndi mapindi zisanu pa galimoto
Do I need my passport?	Kodi ndizafunika chitupa?

PUBLIC TRANSPORT

Is this the right bus for…?	Kodi iyi ndiyo basi yopita ku..?
Where's the nearest bus stop?	Basi stopu yapafupi ndi iti?
How much is the fare?	Ndizingati kulipila?
I'm going to…	Ndiyenda pa…
Where can I drop off?	Ndinga selukile kuti?
Which bus/train can I take to..?	Ndiyiti basi/sitima yaku…?
Can I have my change?	Munganipaseko chenji yanga?
Please stop here	Imani pano

CARS

I want to hire a car	Ndifunda galimoto yobweleka
Where's the best place to rent a car?	Ndingabweleke kuti galimoto?
I want a small/large vehicle	Ndifuna galimoto ing'ono/ikulu
I want it today/tomorrow	Ndifuna lelo/mawa
How much do you charge?	Mulipilisa zingati?
Fill it up please	Zuli kizani
The tyre's flat	Thaila ya pompoloka
It's broken down	Ndiyakufa

Can you fix it?	Mungakonze?
Is there a garage/mechanic near here?	Kodi pali galaji/olungisa pano?
When will it be ready?	Izakonzedwa liti?
Can you do it now?	Munga chite manje?

GAME VIEWING

We want to go somewhere on Friday	Ndifuna kupita kwina pa chisanu
There'll be two of us	Tizhakhala awiri
Is it worth seeing?	Nzokondwelesa kuona?
Is it suitable for children?	Kodi ana anga wone?
How much does it cost?	Zingati?
What does the price include?	Kodi mtengo ukwana chani na chani?
What time will we leave?	Tiima nthawi bwanji?
What time will we get back?	Tibwelako nthawi bwanji?
Is lunch included?	Kudya kwamuzuwa kukhalako?
Where do I buy a ticket?	Ndizagula kuti tikiti?
Buffalo	Njati
Crocodile	Ng'ona
Elephant	Njobvu
Giraffe	Nyamalikiti
Hippopotamus	Mvuu
Lion	Mukango
Monkey	Nyani
Rhinoceros	Chipembele
Snake	Njoka
Zebra	Mbizi

AT THE HOTEL

I want a good hotel	Ndifuna hotela yabwino
Do you have a room available?	Malo aliko?
I want a room for… people	Ndifuna chipinda chanthu…
With a nice view	Kooneka bwino
For one night/two nights/ one week	Usiku umodzi/masiku awiri/ sabata limodzi
I've made a reservation	Ndasungisa malo pa
My name is…	Dzina langa ndine…
How much is a room?	Kodi chipinda dzingati?
Is breakfast included?	Chakudya cham'mawa chilimo?
Is it air conditioned?	Muli moya wokwana ndi conditioner?
You are in room number…	Muli muchipinda chanambala..
Please give me a wake-up call at..	Mundidzusepa…
Is there a restaurant here?	Kuli modyela muno?
Is there a…	Kodi kuli…
Swimming pool	Swimming pool
Gym	Gym
Hairdressers	Salon
Gift shop	Sitolo yamphaso
Night club	Komwela ndi kuvina
Business centre	Malo amalonda
Please bring my luggage	Bweletsani katundu yanga
Are there any messages for me?	Kodi kuli uthenga wanga?
I want bed and breakfast only	Ndifuna pogona ndi chakudya cham'mwawa
I want lunch included	Ndifuna muonjeze chakudya chamuzuwa

Porter	Porter
Please help with my bags	Ndi thandizeni ndi mabagi
It's heavy	Nicholema
Please fetch me a taxi	Ndipezeleni taxi

SHOPPING

At the…	Ku…
Market	M'sika
Shop	Sitolo
Grocers	Sitolo lo galumo zosiyana-siyana
Chemist	Sitolo la mankwala
Gift shop	Sitolo la mphaso
I want one	Ndifuna chimozi
Give me this/these, please	Ndipatseni ichi/izi
How much is it?	Dzingati?
That's too expensive	Nchodula
Can you lower the price?	Bwezanikoni
Have you got anything cheaper?	Kodi muli ndi zochipako?
It's nice/beautiful	Ndi chabwino
I like it	Ndikonda
I don't like it	Sindicikonda ici
Yes, please	Inde
No, thank you	Iyai
Do you sell…?	Kodi mugulisa…?
Here's the money	Iyi ndalama
Have you got change for this?	Kodi muli ndi chenji?
Please can I have my change?	Ndipatseni chenji?
I'll buy it	Ndigula
How many?	Ndi angati?

I don't have enough money	Ndiribe ndalama
It's too big/small	Nchikulu/ndika ng'ono
Do you have it in my size?	Kodi muli ndi saizi yanga?
Do you have it in this colour?	Kodi mui ndi mutundu uyu?
I want a/some…	Ndifunako…
Can I try this/these on?	Kodi ndinga yesemo?
I need a receipt	Ndifuna reciept

Sometimes you can swap things for goods, e.g. a t-shirt could be used as part payment towards a souvenir.

AT THE POST OFFICE

Where is the Post Office?	Kodi ndikuti kuli Post Office?
How much is a stamp for…?	Ndizingati stamp…?
I want to send this letter/ parcel to…	Ndifuna nditumize kalata/ katundu ku…
Five stamps for letters/ postcards to… please	Masitampa asanu amakalata/ ma postcards-kupita ku…
Where can I post them?	Ndinga tu mizire kutima kalata?
Please give me an airmail envelope	Ndipasileniko envelopu ya airmail
Do you sell airmail writing paper?	Mugulisa mapepala a airmail olembapo kodi?

IN A RESTAURANT/CAFÉ

I want a table for… people	Ndifuna thebulo la anthu…
Near the window	Pafupi ndi window
I want to eat…	Ndifuna kudya…
I want to drink…	Ndifuna kumwa…

Breakfast	Chakudya chamawa
Lunch	Chakudya chamudzuwa
Dinner	Chakudya chamadzulo
Snack	Snack
What's the speciality?	Nzabwanji zabwino?
What do you recommend?	Kodi munga sankhe iti?
Knife	M'peni
Fork	Foloko
Spoon	Sipuni
Plate	Mbale
Cup	Kapu
Glass	Glasi
Dish	Mbale
I've made a reservation	Ndasunga malo
My name is…	Dzina langa ndine…
That's not what I ordered	Sindina tumize izo
Dinner is ready	Chakudya chakonzedwa
Can I have some more of this, please?	Kodi mungathe kundi pasa zina?
Can I see the menu/wine list?	Kodi ndinga wone mun dandanda waza kudya/wine?
I'd like to have a…	Ndifuna kukhala ndi…
What drinks do you have?	Kodi ndizakumwa zotani zimene muli nazo?
Where can I get a drink?	Kodi ndingazipeze kuti zakumwa-kumwa?
Would you like tea or coffee?	Kodi mufuna tiyi kapena khofi?
I'll have a beer please	Ndizafuna mowa
One cup of coffee	Kapu ya khofi
Cheers!	Mwani bwino!

Can I have some salt, please	Mundipasileko munyu
This is delicious	Izi nzokoma
I don't want anything else	Sindifuna china chili chonse
The bill, please	Tifuna bilu

FOOD AND DRINK

Food	Chakudya
Coffee	Khofi
Tea	Tiyi
Beer	Mowa
Water	Mandzi
Beef	Nyama ya ng'ombe
Pork	Nyama ya nkumba
Chicken	Nkuku
Fish	Nsomba
Maize	Chimanga
Tomato	Chimate
Okra	Delele
Pumpkin leaves	Chibwabwa
Beans	Kaela
Rice	M'punga
Sweet potato	Kandolo
Onion	Anyenzi
Salt	M'chele
Sugar	Suga
Cold	Kudzidzila
Hot	Kupya
Sweet	Kutsekemela
Spicy	Zonunkhila

The staple food in Zambia is nshima*, made with mealie meal, served with relish and eaten with your hands.*

GETTING HELP

Help!	Nthandizeni!
Call the police	Itanani apolisi!
I need an ambulance	Ndifuna ambulance
I feel ill	Ndimvela kudwala
I've been robbed	Andibela
I need a doctor	Ndifuna sin'ganga
My… hurts	…anga uwawa
Head	Mutu
Stomach	M'mimba
Arm	Dzanja
Leg	Mwendo
Back	M'sana
It hurts here	Chiwawa apa
I can't sleep	Sindigona
I'm feeling worse	Ndimvera kuipa kopitilila
I'm feeling better	Ndimvera bwino
Take me to the…	Ndi tengeni ku…
Hospital	Chipitala
Doctor	Dotolo
Police	Mtsilikali
I've lost my passport	Chanditaika chitupa
My money's been stolen	Ndalama zanga zabedwa
I left it in my room/on the bus	Ndina siya muchipinda/mu basi
Is there someone who can help me?	Kodi kungakhale wondithandiza?

It's an emergency	Ndizo fulumiza
We need help urgently	Tifuna thandizo msanga
Call the police/ambulance/ fire brigade	Itani atsilikali/ambulance/ afire brigade
Where are you?	Muli ali kuti?
I'm at…	Ndiri pa…
What's happened?	Nchani chachitika?
There's been an accident/a fire	Kwachitika ngozi/moto
It's serious	Zili serious

To call for help, dial 999 and state which sort of assistance you require.

DAYS, TIME AND WEATHER

Monday	Lolemba
Tuesday	Chiwiri
Wednesday	Chitatu
Thursday	Chinai
Friday	Chisanu
Saturday	Chiwelu
Sunday	Lamulungu
Today	Lelo
Yesterday	Dzulo
Tomorrow	Mawa
Last week	Sabata latha
Last month	Mwezi watha
Last year	Chaka chatha
Next week	Sabata lamawa
Next month	Mwezi wamawa
Next year	Chaka chamawa

Morning	M'mawa
Afternoon	Masana
Evening	Madzulo
Night	Usiku
See you tomorrow!	Tidza onana mawa!
See you on Friday!	Tidza onana pachisanu!
Now	Tsopano
Then	Ndipo
Later	Patsogolo pache
Before	Sanafike
After	Pambuyo pake
What time is it?	Nthawi ili bwanji?
It's… o'clock	Ili… koloko (you can say the number in English)

Zambia uses the twenty-four clock in telling the time, e.g. 6pm – 18:00 hours.

What's the weather like?	Kwacha bwanji?
It's hot	Kwapya
It's cold	Kwazizila
It's rainy	Mvula iloka
It's windy	Kuli mphepo yambiri

NUMBERS AND MONEY

One	Imodzi
Two	Awiri
Three	Atatu
Four	Anai
Five	Asanu
Six	Zisanu ndi chimodzi
Seven	Zisanu ndi ziwiri
Eight	Zisanu ndi zitatu
Nine	Zisanu ndi zinai
Ten	Khumi

For higher numbers, use English.
The Zambian currency is Kwacha and Ngwee.

VERBS

To be	**Kuli**
I am	Ndiri
You (familiar/single) are	Uli
S/he is	Ali
We are	Tiri
You (polite/plural) are	Muli
They are	Ali
To have	**Kuli ndi**
I have	Ndiri ndi
You (familiar/single) have	Uli ndi
S/he has	Ali ndi
We have	Tiri ndi
You (polite/plural) have	Muli ndi
They have	Ali ndi
To want	**Kufuna**
I want	Ndifuna
You (familiar/single) want	Ufuna
S/he wants	Afuna
We want	Tifuna
You (polite/plural) want	Mufuna
They want	Afuna

To like	**Kukonda**
I like	Ndikonda
You (familiar/single) like	Ukonda
S/he likes	Akonda
We like	Tikonda
You (polite/plural) like	Mukonda
They like	Akonda

VERB LIST

To go	Kupita
To come	Kubwela
To eat	Kudya
To drink	Kumwa
To sleep	Kugona
To walk	Kuyenda
To buy	Kugula
To see	Kuona
To stay	Kukhala
To stop	Kuima
To travel	Kuyenda
To pay	Kulipila
To choose	Kusanka
To help	Kuthandiza
To cook	Kuphika
To rest	Kupumula
To feel	Kumvela
To speak	Kulankhula
To give	Kupatsa
To ask	Kufunsa

To know	Kudziwa
To think	Kuganiza
To be happy	Kukondwera

TONGA

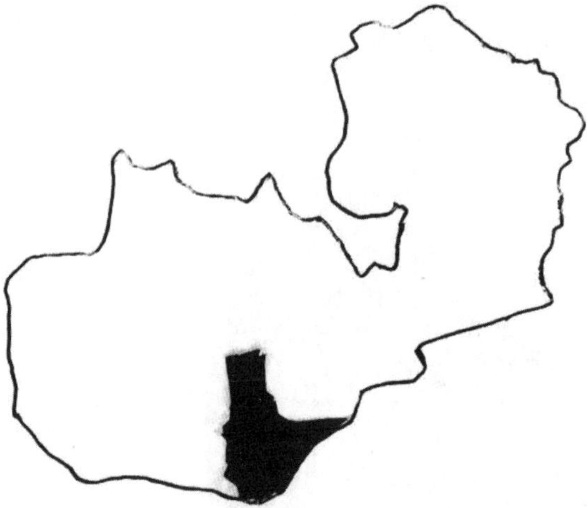

The Tonga-speaking people of Zambia live mainly in the Southern Province.

'Kabuca uleta tunji'
Tomorrow brings many things

GREETINGS AND FIRST WORDS

Hello	Wabonwa
How are you?	Muli buti?
I'm fine. And you?	Ndikabotu. Chita ndiwe?
Fine, thank you	Ndikabotu, ndalumba
Good morning	Mwabuka buti
Good afternoon	Mwalibizya buti
Good night	Kudiye kabotu
Goodbye	Muchale kabotu
See you!	Tulabonana
Yes	Ee
No	Pepe
Maybe	Andiza
Okay/fine	Mbubo/kabotu
Excuse me	Amundijatile/ndalomba
Sorry	Chabija
Thank you very much	Twalumba kapati
What's your name?	Ndiwe ni izyina?
My name is…	Izyina lyangu ndime…
Pleased to meet you	Ndalumba kubonana andiwe
Please come in	Kamunjila
Please sit down	Kamukala
Welcome	Watambulwa
Please can you help me?	Hena inga mwandigwasha?

Who?	Nguni?
What?	Nchizi?
Where?	Nkuli?
When?	Ndilili?
Why?	Inokayi?
Which?	Nchili?
How?	Mbubuti?

To show respect, preface the name of the person you are talking to with 'Ba', e.g. May – Ba Mary; Mr Phiri – Ba Phiri.

GENERAL CONVERSATION

Do you speak English?	Hena ulakanana cikuwa?
I don't speak Tonga	Hekanani chitonga
I speak a little Tonga	Ndakanana ashonto chitonga
I am learning Tonga	Ndalayiya chitonga
Sorry, I don't understand	Ndijatile tanditeleli
Please repeat that	Koindululka echo
Please speak slowly	Ikaka kwamba asyontosyonto
What is this?	Nchinzi echi?
How do you say… in Tonga?	Ino wambabuti… muchintonga?
How do you say… in English?	Ino wambabuti… mu chikuwa?
Did I pronounce it right?	Hena nda amba kabotu?
Do you understand me?	Hena ulanditelelea mebo?
This is my…	Echi nchi changu…
Wife	Mukaintu ukwetwe
Husband	Mulumi ukwete
Son	Mwana musankwa

Daughter	Mwana musimbi
Sister	Muchizyi muchizyi
Brother	Munyina ndumi
Friend	Mwenzuma
Family	Mukwanti
I work as a…	Ndabeleka mulimo wa…
I am… years old	Ndijisi myaka yakuzyalwa ili...
Are you married?	Hena ulikwete?
I am married	Ndili kwete
I am not married	Tandikwete
How many children do you have?	Ino ujisi bana bongaye?
I don't have any children	Tandi jisi nikuba bana
I have… children	Ndi jisi bana…
I am on holiday	Ndili amazuba akulyokezya
I am working here	Ndabeleka ano
I live here	Ndikala wano
Where do you come from?	Mwazwa kuli?
I am from…	Ndazwa ku…
Can I take a photo?	Hena ndakozya kubweza chifwanikiso?
Where is the toilet?	Kuli kuli chimbuzi?
Entrance	Kumanjililo
Exit	Kwakuzwida
Ladies	Bamakaintu
Gentlemen	Balume
Me	Mebo
You	Webo
She	Mukaintu
He	Musankwa
We	Swebo

They	Balo
I feel cold/hot	Ndafwa mpeyo/kupya
I feel tired	Ndakatala
I am hungry and thirsty	Ndafwa nzala anyota
I like it here	Ndachiyanda ano
Mr	Mulombwana
Mrs	Bamuka
Miss	Mukaintu
See you later	Ndakubona kabotu
See you tomorrow	Ndakubona chifumo
Why?	Inokayi?
Because…	Nkaambo…
I don't understand	Tanditeleli
I don't know	Tandizyi
I think…	Ndayeya kuti…
I want…	Ndayanda…
I don't want…	Nsiyandi…
I like…	Ndayanda…
I don't like…	Nsichiyandi…

GETTING AROUND

Excuse me, where is…?	Nkuli chili kuli…?
Where are the…?	Ziki kuli…?
Shops	Tuntoolo
Restaurants	Akulida
Night clubs	Manda a kuli komanisha masiku
Where is the…?	Ino chili kuli…?
Lake	Lwiizyi
River	Mulonga

Village	Munzi
Game park	Kuhubailwa banyama
Post Office	Kutumu mali na magwalo
Bank	Ibanga
Bureau de Change	Kuchinchilwa mali
Museum	Nganda ya hintu nhya nsiku
Church	Chikombelo
Bus stop	Kutautilusa mabhasi
Train station	Kutautilusa chitima
Airport	Bbuwa lyandeke
Where is this?	Chili kuli echi?
Can I walk there?	Hena ingandenda amaulu?
Do you have a map?	Sa ulijisi chitondezyo?
Can you show me?	Hena ulakozya kunditondezya ime?
To the…	Kuli ba…
Left	Kulumwesyi
Right	Kululyo
Straight ahead	Kumblele utanyoni
Where are you going?	Ino uya kuli?
I am going to…	Ndiya ku…
Is this the way to…?	Hena ninzila eyi…?
I want to travel by…	Ndiyanda kweenjda a…
Bicycle	Namutendele
Motorbike	Mudududu
Boat	Bwato
Horse	Ibiza
Vehicle (general)	Mootokala
How much does the journey cost?	Ino lweendo lutola mali ongaye?
How long will it take?	Ino libola chiindi chilanhu buti?

Can I buy a ticket?	Hena ndakozya kula dickiti?
Where's the bus/train/ plane/boat for…?	Ino nkuli kuli ibbasi/citima/ indeke/bwato zya…
How can I go there?	Ino inga ndaunka buti kuya?
I want to see the…	Ndiyanda kubona…
Is there a driver?	Hena kwali namutekenya?
Can I go today?	Hena inga ndaunka sunu?
Is there an entrance fee?	Hena nkubadela kunjila?
What are the opening hours?	Maola buti akujalulila?
It's open from… to…	Ilajulwa kutalikila… kusikila...
Street/road	Mugwagwa
A little bit	Ashoonto buyo
A lot	Zinji
Quickly	Fwambana
Slowly	Asyoontosyonto
What's the best way to…?	Njili inzila kwiinola ibotu ku..?
Should I take a taxi?	Ino ndibweze motokala?
It's near the …	Mpafwafwi a…
Cross the road	Kuso toka mugwagwa
Go past the…	Koya kwiindililei…
It's near here	Nkufwafwi akokuno
It's far from here	Nkulamfu kuzwa wano
It's too far to walk	Nkulamfu maningi kweenda amaulu
It's ten minutes by foot	Maola nali kumi amaulu
It's five minutes by car	Tuhwalu tosamwe amootokala
Do I need my passport?	Hena ndayanda chitupa changu?

PUBLIC TRANSPORT

Is this the right bus for…?	Hena eyi ndi basi ili iunka ku..?
Where's the nearest bus stop?	Nkuli kufwafwi kutantila mabasi?
How much is the fare?	Nku badalwa mali ogayi?
I'm going to…	Ndaunka ku…
Where can I drop off?	Ino inga ndaselukila kuli?
Which bus/train can I take to…?	Njili basi/chitima chinga chandi tola oku?
Can I have my change?	Kamundipa mali angu achaala?
Please stop here	Kamuima ano

CARS

I want to hire a car	Ndiyanda kubbuking'a motokala
Where's the best place to rent a car?	Nkuli kutusena tubotu kule ntin wa motokala?
I want a small/large vehicle	Ndi yanda mushonto/mupati motokala
I want it today/tomorrow	Ndiyanda sunu/chifumo
How much do you charge?	Ino mubadelesya buti?
Fill it up please	Amuchizuzyekaka
The tyre's flat	Hwili lyaponcha
It's broken down	Mootokala wahwa
Can you fix it?	Hena inga wa u bamba?
Is there a garage/mechanic near here?	Hena kuli a bambilwa na u bamba myootokalaa hwaahwi akokuno?
When will it be ready?	Ndilili ndinga yaba kabotu?
Can you do it now?	Hena ulakozya kucicita ono?

GAME VIEWING

We want to go somewhere on Friday	Tuyanda kuunka kumbi mu mujibelo
There'll be two of us	Tuya kuba tobilo
Is it worth seeing?	Hena chilakondelezya?
Is it suitable for children?	Hena nchibotu kubana?
How much does it cost?	Ino chuulwa malinzi?
What does the price include?	Ino mu muuto muli anzi?
What time will we leave?	Ino tulanyamuka chindinzi?
What time will we get back?	Tulajoka chindinzi?
Is lunch included?	Sa cakulya ca cilu ngulungu cili bikilwe?
Where do I buy a ticket?	Nkuli nko ndinga ndaula dikiti?
Buffalo	Munyati
Crocodile	Chiwena
Elephant	Muzovu
Giraffe	Indyabuluba
Hippopotamus	Chivubwe
Lion	Shumbwa
Monkey	Sokwe
Snake	Nzoka
Rhinoceros	Chipembele
Zebra	Chibize

AT THE HOTEL

I want a good hotel	Ime ndayanda ibotu hotelo
Do you have a room available?	He nkoili nganda yakoona?
I want a room for… people	Nganda ikwana bantu bali bo...

With a nice view	Iijisi buse bwakulingila aabotu
For one night/two nights/ one week	Ya busiku bomwe/masiku obile/ nsondo yomwe
I've made a reservation	Ndamu hyibya kale kuti ndayanda nganda
My name is…	Izina lyangu ndime…
How much is a room?	Hena nganda ibbadelwa buti?
Is breakfast included?	Hena chakulya chamafumo chilibikilwe?
Is it air conditioned?	Hena mulainda muya mubotu?
You are in room number…	Uli muuganda iitwa kuti…
Please give me a wake-up call at	Hikaaka mundibushe ciindi ca..
Is there a restaurant here?	Hena nkoili aano ng'anda ya kulida aawo?
Is there a…	Hena nkocili chi…
Swimming pool	Chiziba cisambilwa
Gym	Mwakusobanina
Hairdressers	Kubumbilwa masusu
Gift shop	Kuulwa zipeyo
Night club	Kwakuli komanishya masiku
Business centre	Kujanika milimo ya mpindu
Room service	Kulida munganda yakoona
Please bring… to my room	Mundiletele… ku n'ganda yangu
Please bring my luggage	Hikaaka mundiletele mukuli wanga
Are there any messages for me?	Hena kulimilumbe yangu?
I want bed and breakfast only	Ndiyanda bulo a cisunsulo hyalo
I want lunch included	Ndayanda cakulya cacilungulun gu cicalo mubike
Porter	Shikunyamuna

Please help with my bags	Amandingwashe ahibbeke hyangu
It's heavy	Nchilemu
Please fetch me a taxi	Ndakomba kamundiyandawida moota

SHOPPING

At the…	Ku…
Market	Musika
Shop	Chintoolo
Grocers	Chintoolo
Chemist	Mujanwa misamu yandene
Gift shop	Muuzyilwa zipeyo
I want one	Ndiyanda comwe
Give me this/these, please	Amundipe ime echi/ezyi ikaka
How much is it?	Mbubuti echi?
That's too expensive	Chiladula
Can you lower the price?	Hena inga tamujoli mulo?
Have you got anything cheaper?	Hena uli jisi chimwi chitaduli?
It's nice/beautiful	Echi nchibotu/chilebeleka
I like it	Ndachiyanda echi
I don't like it	Echi hechiyandi
Yes, please	Ee, kaka
No, thank you	Pepe, ndalumba
Do you sell…?	Hena mula uzya…?
Here's the money	Ngaya mali
Have you got change for this?	Sa mulijisi chakuchincha
Please can I have my change?	Amundipe chanji yangu kaka?
I'll buy it	Ndila chula echi

How many?	Zyongaye?
I don't have enough money	Hejisi mali manji akwana
It's too big/small	Nchipati maningi/nchisonto
Do you have it in my size?	Hena muli chijisi chikwana ndime?
Do you have it in this colour?	Hena muli chijisi mumubala oyu?
I want a/some...	Ndayanda...
Can I try this/these on?	Hena ndisole echi/eehyo?
I need a receipt	Ndiyanda lisiti

Sometimes you can swap things for goods, e.g. a t-shirt could be used as part payment towards a souvenir.

AT THE POST OFFICE

Where is the Post Office?	Ino nkukuli kutambwidwa mag walo?
How much is a stamp for...?	Chamba mali ongaye...?
I want to send this letter/ parcel to...	Ndiyanda kutuma olulugwalo/ chibudu ku...
Five stamps for letters/postcards to... please	Hi tamba hyo sanwe hya mangwato/ma card...
Where can I post them?	Ino inga ndatumizya kuli ezyo?
Please give me an airmail envelope	Ndalomba nhulupu iiyenda aandeke
Do you sell airmail writing paper?	Hena mula ulishya mapepa akulembela a tumwa a ndeke?

IN A RESTAURANT/CAFÉ

I want a table for… people	Ndiyanda tabule yabantu…
Near the window	Afwafwi ampulumwido
I want to eat…	Ndiyanda kulya…
I want to drink…	Ndiyanda kunwa…
Breakfast	Musuzulo
Lunch	Cakulya acilungulungu
Dinner	Cakulya chamasiku
Snack	Twakuhya
What's the speciality?	Nchomuchizhi kabatu ku jika nchinzi?
What do you recommend?	Ino nchinzi ncho lombozya?
Knife	Chipeni
Fork	Holoko
Spoon	Mungo
Plate	Mutiba
Cup	Nkomeki
Glass	Glazi
Dish	Mutiba mupati
I've made a reservation	Nda yo bozya
My name is…	Izyina lyangundime…
That's not what I ordered	Echi tachihi nchinda yooohya
Dinner is ready	Camana cakulya kabambwa
Can I have some more of this, please?	Hena inga nsijani cimbi akaka?
Can I see the menu/wine list?	Amundipe chipepa cilembedwe tusiwa/chakulya?
I'd like to have a…	Ndilayanda kuba a…
What drinks do you have?	Ino nchakunywanzi nchojisi?

Where can I get a drink?	Nkuli nkonda tandajana chakunywa?
Would you like tea or coffee?	Hena inga wayanda tiyi na kofi?
I'll have a beer please	Ndilanywa bukoko
One cup of coffee	Nkomeki yomwe ya kofi
Cheers!	Ndalumba!
Can I have some salt, please	Sa unga nsijani mwino
This is delicious	Cilaina ceci
I don't want anything else	Tandiyandi cimbi kunze a ceeci
The bill, please	Cipepa cibadehya mali aakubadela

FOOD AND DRINK

Food	Chakulya
Coffee	Kofi
Tea	Tii
Beer	Bukoko
Water	Meenda
Beef	Nyama yangombe
Pork	Nyama ya ngulube
Chicken	Nyama ya nkuku
Fish	Inswi
Maize	Mapopwe
Tomato	Ideede
Okra	Lunkomba
Pumpkin leaves	Lungu
Beans	Bunyangu
Rice	Laisi

Sweet potato	Cimbwali
Onion	Hangisi
Salt	Munyo
Sugar	Chuka
Cold	Kutontola
Hot	Kupya
Sweet	Kulweela
Spicy	Kupya mukwamwa

The staple food in Zambia is nshima*, made with mealie meal, served with relish and eaten with your hands.*

GETTING HELP

Help!	Ndigwashe!
Call the police	Amwite ba pulisa!
I need an ambulance	Ndayanda moota uunyamuna balwazi
I feel ill	Ndaciswa
I've been robbed	Ndabidwa
I need a doctor	Ndiyanda musilisi
My… hurts	…cilacisa
Head	Mutwe
Stomach	Mwida
Arm	Janza
Leg	Kulu
Back	Kushule
It hurts here	Cicisa wawa
I can't sleep	Tandikozyi koona

I'm feeling worse	Ndalimvwa kwindilila
I'm feeling better	Ndalimvwa katobu
Take me to the…	Amundi tole ku…
Hospital	Cibadela
Doctor	Musilisi
Police	Ma pulisa
I've lost my passport	Ndasowa citupa cangu
My money's been stolen	Mali angu abigwa
I left it in my room/on the bus	Ndacisiya mung'andu yangu/ mu moota
Is there someone who can help me?	Hena inga kulaba unga ulandig washa?
It's an emergency	Nchalubilo
We need help urgently	Tulayanda kugwashigwa chakufwambana
Call the police/ambulance/ fire brigade	Amwiite mapulisa/amota abweza baciswa/auzimamulilo
Where are you?	Ino uli kuli?
I'm at…	Ndili ku…
What's happened?	Nchinzi chacitika?
There's been an accident/a fire	Kwali ntenda/amulilo
It's serious	Chili sinizyide

To call for help, dial 999 and state which sort of assistance you require.

DAYS, TIME AND WEATHER

Monday	Mumuhulo
Tuesday	Bwatalu
Wednesday	Bwane
Thursday	Bwasanu
Friday	Mujibelo
Saturday	Munsabbata
Sunday	Munsondo
Today	Sunu
Yesterday	Ijilo
Tomorrow	Chifumo
Last week	Nsondo yamana
Last month	Mwezi wamana
Last year	Mwaka wamana
Next week	Nsondo iboola
Next month	Mwezi ubola
Next year	Mwaka ubola
Morning	Mafumofumo
Afternoon	Masikati
Evening	Mangolezya
Night	Masiku
See you tomorrow!	Tulabonana chifumo!
See you on Friday!	Tulabonana mumujibelo!
Now	Ono
Then	Eelyo
Later	Akale
Before	Kotana
After	Wamana

What time is it?	Ino nchindi nzi?
It's… o'clock	Camich a…

Zambia uses the twenty-four clock in telling the time, e.g. 6pm – 18:00 hours.

What's the weather like?	Ino luoluli buti?
It's hot	Kulapya
It's cold	Kulatontola
It's rainy	Kuli nhhula
It's windy	Kuli muo

NUMBERS AND MONEY

One	Komwe
Two	Tobile
Three	Totatwe
Four	Tone
Five	Tosanwe
Six	Chisambome
Seven	Chiloba
Eight	Lusele
Nine	Ifuka
Ten	Kumi

For higher numbers, use English.
The Zambian currency is Kwacha and Ngwee.

VERBS

To be	**Kuba**
I am	Ndime
You (familiar/single) are	Uli
S/he is	Uli
We are	Ndiswe
You (polite/plural) are	Muli
They are	Bali
To have	**Ku**
I have	Ndijisi
You (familiar/single) have	Ujisi
S/he has	Ujisi
We have	Tulijisi
You (polite/plural) have	Mulijisi
They have	Balijisi
To want	**Ku**
I want	Ndayanda
You (familiar/single) want	Uyanda
S/he wants	Uyanda
We want	Tulayanda
You (polite/plural) want	Mulayanda
They want	Balayanda

To like	**Ku**
I like	Ndayanda
You (familiar/single) like	Ulayanda
S/he likes	Ulayanda
We like	Tulayanda
You (polite/plural) like	Mulayanda
They like	Balayanda

VERB LIST

To go	Kuunka
To come	Kuboola
To eat	Kulya
To drink	Kunywa
To sleep	Koona
To walk	Kweenda
To buy	Kuula
To see	Kubona
To stay	Kusyala
To stop	Kwiima
To travel	Kweenda
To pay	Kubadela
To choose	Kusala
To help	Kugwasha
To cook	Kujika
To rest	Kupumula
To feel	Kuhwa
To speak	Kwambaula
To give	Kupa
To ask	Kubuzya

To know	Kuhiba
To think	Kuyeya
To be happy	Kukomana

OTHER LANGUAGES SPOKEN IN ZAMBIA

Ambo
Aushi
Bisa
Chewa
Chinamukulu
Chishinga
Cokwe
Goba
Ila
Iwa
Kabanga
Kololo
Kunda
Lala
Lamba
Lima
Lenje
Luchazi
Lungu
Makololo
Mambwe
Mashi
Mbunda
Namwanga
Ndebele
Ndembu
Ngoni
Nkoya
Nsenga
Nyiha
Sala
Seba
Shona
Simaa
Soli
Swahili
Swaka
Tabwa
Tambo
Totela
Tumbuka
Unga
Ushi